RUN STEADY RUN STRAIGHT

RUN STEADY RUN STRAIGHT

HOW TO ENDURE IN THE MARATHON OF LIFE

KNUTE LARSON

Formerly titled *The Great Human Race*

VICTOR BOOKS®
A DIVISION OF SCRIPTURE PRESS PUBLICATIONS INC.
USA CANADA ENGLAND

Unless otherwise indicated, Scripture quotations are from the *New American Standard Bible*, © the Lockman Foundation 1960, 1962, 1963, 1968, 1971, 1972, 1973, 1975, 1977. Others are from the *King James Version* (KJV); the *Holy Bible, New International Version* (NIV), © 1973, 1978, 1984, International Bible Society. Used by permission of Zondervan Bible Publishers; and *The Living Bible* (TLB), © 1971, Tyndale House Publishers, Wheaton, IL 60189. Used by permission.

Recommended Dewey Decimal Classification: 248.4
Suggested Subject Heading: CHRISTIAN LIVING

Library of Congress Catalog Card Number: 87-81017
ISBN: 0-89693-824-7

Printed in the United States of America.

For information, address Victor Books, Wheaton, IL 60187.

CONTENTS

Dedicated to my running partner,

Jeanine.

Friend-wife.

May we tie.

WARMUP

One coach at a recent Olympics commented on the marvelous athletes competing there and said that the difference in those who take home the gold and the others is "the size of their 'wanna.' "

Their want to.

Their willpower.

This book is about that, and how it relates to the strength of God in our lives.

For the daily run.

I am reminded of this every time I watch the beginning of "Wide World of Sports" Saturday afternoons on television. It always starts with fabulous action scenes from competition and announcer Jim McKay saying in the background, "The thrill of victory . . . the agony of defeat."

As he speaks of defeat, a downhill skier is shown losing control at the bottom of a ski jump, then falling in a discombobulated heap.

The poor guy has to do it again every Saturday afternoon! ("OK, Charlie, it's time to do it again"—can't you hear it?)

The agony of defeat—who has not felt it?

But there is also agony in victory.

Winners agonize.

And so do runners who stay at it.

Some runners look like runners. They appear as if they were carved from a sleek model of a Boston Marathon champion. They jog or run, it seems to the watcher, almost effortlessly.

For me, it is mostly agony. My build must have been for basketball perhaps, though I lack unusual height.

Or maybe for centerfield, where I tried my days in Little League and later college baseball.

Perhaps checkers is what I was built for.

But anyway, I must run.

Build or no build.

Ease or no ease.

The alarm is off and the day has begun. Here we go!

"The race is not to the swift," Solomon moans (Ecc. 9:11). Overall, life is not fair. Spiritual justice awaits its day.

But often the swift win the leg races. Those who have trained well run well.

So we buffet our bodies (1 Cor. 9:27).

That means we "black-and-blue" our spirits to get them to listen to higher orders and do what is best in the long run.

And the long run is really what this life is all about. It's not the pleasantries I exchanged with my bride at the wedding service, or how creative were our homemade covenants; it's what I was saying to my Jeanine these last few days, after more than twenty-five years together.

It's not how my testimony sparkled when I first gave it after receiving Christ as Saviour, but what kind of shine has been in my life during the pressure times of the last few months.

The great human race is a marathon. Sprinters die young. Faithfulness doesn't even count until a while later.

This book is about endurance, the twin of commitment.

It is about "remaining under," as the Greeks liked to think of endurance. It's about the size of your "wanna."

Part of remaining under and wanting to win is buffeting your body. If we translated that for today's American luxury world, most would understand that word to mean a line we go through at a neighborhood restaurant.

We do that too much.

If you are already eighty years in Christ and close to the

finish line, you probably do not need the advice I offer in this book.

But if you are running at the beginning or middle of the race and, like me, you appreciate when someone cheers you on and yells, "You can do it," then this book is for you.

One for the run.

KNUTE LARSON
Akron, Ohio
1987

1

FIRST LAP

"Do you not know that those who run in a race all run, but only one receives the prize? Run in such a way that you may win. And everyone who competes in the games exercises self-control in all things. They then do it to receive a perishable wreath, but we an imperishable. Therefore I run in such a way, as not without aim; I box in such a way, as not beating the air; but I buffet my body and make it my slave, lest possibly, after I have preached to others, I myself should be disqualified."

(1 Cor. 9:24-27)

I like to run.

I don't like to run.

I learned to live with ambivalence when I was little, so I can claim both statements.

Most of us who believe Jesus is Lord and Universe Master like to be counted among His followers.

But we also buck the system and like to do things our own way—a nice way to say we lust in the flesh. If we didn't like to think selfish thoughts, we wouldn't think them so much. If vengeful thoughts were not the least bit entertaining, we probably would not have them in for a party so often.

We choose.

Romans 7, with its annoying ambivalence, covers us all: we want to do right, but we don't; we don't want to do wrong, but we do.

To admit that is not shame.

Neither is it the end.

Instead it should be the start of our search for strength and consistency, for help in the long haul.

The human will is more complicated than I can describe, but for sure I know that content alone does not change it. Otherwise, the thousands of Christian-school grads would all be virile models of Christian action and secular-sacred integration. Every graduate of a Christian home would pass the torch carefully and with the same finesse and content.

But it is not that way.

Facts about car safety may have persuaded a few people to wear seat belts, but the law buckled up many more.

Let's face it—we make many of our decisions by will and emotion power alone. "Don't confuse me with the facts—I've already made up my mind" is not just a cute saying.

It is often the way we live.

That's why living the best life—trusting in and obeying God by following His Son Jesus Christ—is recognizing what daily decisions need to follow the biggest one, when we received Him as Saviour and Lord.

I did not become a robot disciple after my conversion. In fact, it was just the beginning.

A big one for sure, but just the start.

Now for the daily acceptance of Him as Saviour and Lord, as the One to be followed or chosen in the grind we call daily.

He helps us choose the right, and He rewards us with strength as we do.

But we indeed choose.

A close parallel—not a perfect one admittedly—is a race, a marathon. Getting into the race and starting is major, to be sure. You're not even in the race if you're not even in the race!

But entrance is followed by the disciplines of staying on course and continuing.

Such is life, the Christian one. We begin by a choice of faith and we grow by daily choices of faith, taking right over wrong.

So life is no "Let-go-and-let-God" retreat from choices, but a process of learning how God thinks and what pleases Him, then deciding accordingly. Thus is He glorified.

"Work out your own salvation," Paul commands believers in his letter to the Philippians (2:12). It is one of those verses that must never walk around without the one that follows: "For it is God who is at work in you, both to will and to work for His good pleasure" (2:13).

Nice verses, full of challenge and promise.

"You've got it in you—now work it out! Live it out. Let it be a part of all you do.

"As you do, it will be clear that God is giving you grace and strength so that your life pleases Him."

That's a Larson paraphrase, but I think the commentaries will support it.

Many Christians, sadly, would not.

Some are all willpower and self-helps. "Work it out, baby. It was tough today and it will be tough tomorrow, but work at it. You can do it! You are somebody. You have unlimited potential. Possibilities!"

And so this believer draws on his ego power, which often is sufficient but always is dwindling, to gut out each day for Jesus.

It is hardly fun.

Certainly not very supernatural.

On the other hand, other Christians—and I know just as many of these—adopt a near fatalistic "It-is-God-who-works-in-you-so-set-the-will-button-on-cruise-control-and-watch-what-He-does-for-you" attitude.

Let go; let God.

Surely it has a ring to it.

But many "out-Paul" the apostle on this and blame *all* their choices on God and act as if *all* they do is guided by God.

"I am the glove and Christ is the hand," one friend told me.

Better than "The devil made me do it," I'll admit, but still not the best.

Nor is it biblical.

We choose. *We* will.

Otherwise, we do not win the race.

We map out a course to run, but still choose, each step, each day, to continue in the right direction.

We are responsible.

Accountable.

And able, because He gives grace and ability as we choose His way.

Somewhere in the middle of these extremes just described is the magical balance, the Philippians 2:12-13 double truth.

We work; He works.

Or, if you prefer: He works; we work.

The two are married.

And what God has brought together, let no man put asunder.

I was running in one of my first competitive races. Ten kilometers, or 6.2 miles, where my great goal is to finish standing up.

I don't have to beat very many, just make it to the very end.

I started running regularly when my faithful companion-wife, Jeanine, read Kenneth Cooper's argument for twelve minutes a day dedicated to the cardiovascular system. Being in love, and hoping to better my body for the long stretch ahead, and needing all the energy I can get, I tried.

Twelve became twenty, then thirty—daily, and early.

So I entered this race. Might as well.

Midway, a long sloping hill looked like, or at least felt like, Pike's Peak. An old man, maybe seventy, slid past me on my right side. He had a squeegee bottle of water in one hand and honey in the other, and was swigging doses of each as he ran.

I didn't even have a washrag, and not much will left.

Then a woman passed me on my left.

Forgive me, but I have just enough male chauvinism in me to feel I was done at this point. Woman is meant to be the glory of man, the Bible says. Surely that does not allow for beating him in footraces!

Another man started by and I mentioned in defeat, "It's all yours," meaning the rest of the hill and the rest of the race. And the rest of running forever, if he pleased.

But he would not stand for it. Instead he turned to me and said, "No; come on, run with me. You can do it."

I'll never figure how much was adrenaline and how much was pure ego, but I pulled for something that had not been there up to that point in the race.

And it came!

Gradually it came!

"Lean over," he said, as we ran together. "Always lean forward a little up a hill.

"Now take shorter strides."

I did.

"That's it," he said. "Shorter steps and lean a little up a hill. . . . Come on, we can do it."

By some kind of shared motion we ran stride for stride the last few miles, right past the Mary Miller horse farm, up another hill, and onto the college campus where the judges had gone to prepare a finish line for us.

I was even able to stretch it out and finish right beside him with a fabulous kick at the end. We finished strong.

Not many were still there to see our finish, but we did make it!

I turned to thank him, shake his hand, and ask his name.

It seemed nothing to him, and he walked away.

"Who was that masked rider?"

It was a great lesson in spiritual running too, for such is the Christian run.

Christ comes alongside when we are tiring or getting down. He has run this way before. He has been tested in every point that we have. He understands. "Run with me," He says. Or better, "I will help you run and run with you."

It is for us to decide. If we go His way and seek His fellowship and "look unto Jesus," as Hebrews 12:2 commands, we can do it.

There's a spiritual stamina, an invisible grace, but a very felt force, and it gives us character and helps us proceed.

Run.

Run with Him.

John 15 says it with the beautiful parallel of the vine and

the branches. Christ is in us and we are in Him. Feel it or not!

Sometimes I do; sometimes I don't.

But it is true.

Indeed, I love the idea.

Ever since that first experience, whenever I run in 10K races, I find a partner, a comrade toward the middle of the pack, who is willing to exert a little bit and make it to the end with some pride.

I usually find that person about mile four. If it's a woman, my ego gets in the way and I muster all my strength so that she doesn't end up beating me. I remember one race where my midway buddy—a girl—started kidding me about beating a man, making me even more determined.

But she was better.

She won.

That kind of ruins my illustration, but running with someone really can be encouraging. You pick each other up. "Tell me I can do it," I said to one man I just met at mile three. "Tell me I can finish."

"You can finish," he said. It didn't matter that I had given him the words. We finished. Together.

Running with Christ is no mere emotion. I must see Him in the Gospels and walk His way. I must go to the Epistles and see what He's like, what He wants me to do.

I must then, by grace through faith, ask His strength and walk in His Spirit.

So it is that I can go through my day with the sense of His presence. His joy. His forgiveness. And with that invisible force or strength that helps me choose right over wrong, that helps me discipline my body and self-nature.

I loved the movie *Chariots of Fire*. In one scene, Eric Liddell is preaching in a church in Paris, and he asks the congregation, "Where does this strength come from?"

Then he answers with the words of Isaiah: "They that

wait upon the Lord shall renew their strength; they shall mount up with wings as eagles; they shall run, and not be weary; and they shall walk, and not faint" (Isa. 40:31, KJV).

I have known that joy. I have sensed that endurance. He has kept me going.

In the lonely days, He has been my encouragement, often through people, but often simply through His Word or His Spirit.

In the crowded days, He has let me believe that prayers rescue, even gasps that say, "I love You, and I'm sorry that time is so short today."

When I am weak, He has made me strong.

When I am discouraged and looking at life the wrong way, His Word has brought me back.

He has run with me. I can finish.

Part of the process is my disciplined choosing to obey. But basic to that choosing is the knowledge that He is with me, and revealing the way in Scripture.

His Spirit embellishes and empowers my spirit as I walk or run His way.

My part is to buffet or master my body's regular nature by living by the Spirit in me, not just what my body craves.

We've become too easy on ourselves, we Christians. Our Leader never said it would be easy every time we choose.

"Straight and narrow," were His words.

Not all that popular.

"Die to self, and hate the world," He ordered.

Not all that fun.

"Follow Me and I will make you fishers of men," He challenged.

Not all that easy.

"If you wish to be great, be a servant."

Not all that natural.

Yet Jesus lived such a life, died for our sins, and rose again to show that it works.

It is for Christ to give us the spiritual stamina and drive to help us keep going. That happens as we obey.

People who watch from the sidelines, choosing the natural over the spiritual, obeying feeling and whim rather than what they believe, always wonder where all the grace is.

"What's God ever done for me?" a young father challenged me.

His life and family were really messed up—no question about it. By a series of bad, selfish decisions, he had descended to a state of bitterness toward God and embarrassment toward others, especially the church.

I started to answer his question by talking about his lungs, his heart, his apparent salvation at an early age.

But it was obvious he was in no mood to listen to my list.

He is today still wondering where all the grace is, and may be when he dies.

If a lot of it were not our part, why all the choices and lists and warnings in the Bible? God could have just installed a Walkman earphone in every new convert and then said whatever you say to robots each day to get them to do your bidding.

Instead He left us with choices and His Spirit. And even walking in His Spirit is a choice, not a given.

So balance is called for.

We are not alone. We are not on our own.

But neither are we puppets, empowered every second by God's Spirit so we no longer choose or buffet.

Somewhere in the middle is the biblical—balanced and beautiful.

Workable.

Very daily too. And related to accountability.

Accountability is very important in Scripture. Everybody is going to stand in front of Christ and give account of all he has done, whether it be good or bad. There are many, many biblical references to this truth, and many, many people who have forgotten them.

You have to punch the time clock at the end of the day.

You have to give a sales report at the end of the week.

You have to stand in front of the principal with your grades.

However this whole thing transpires—and the Word of God is not clear about how it will happen—the Judgment Seat is going to be a moment of truth.

No one's going to stand there and point to Billy Graham and say, "I'm with him." While there may be reward for sending some offerings to Jerry Falwell, the question will be not what Jerry did, but what I did. What you did.

That's the point of accountability.

Everyone gives account of his own life.

In a race, only one wins.

In this race, everyone can win.

All who are faithful will receive the reward, and all who follow Christ will have the same joy at the end.

The grand plan.

All of us can be in on it.

But it is up to us.

We are accountable.

God did not make a mistake when He compared the Christian life to running. He didn't make any mistakes anywhere, but this one hits you so many times when you struggle to grow in your faith and then go out and try to run and feel all the parallels.

Running is like living for Christ. Living for Christ is like running.

You get tired. You get frustrated. You have to stretch.

But the more you do it, the farther you want to go. And the more you realize how much better you can become.

Our purpose is to know how to live the life or run the race better. Not necessarily faster, but with stronger endurance and growing enthusiasm.

The Egyptians used to teach that the way you will be judged at death is by weighing your heart.

Your will.

Many people will flunk that final test.

I know this ancient Egyptian teaching is not exactly what the Bible says, but I think there's a good lesson there.

God has given us different bodies. Environment has shaped us in different ways. Circumstances have been unfair, it seems.

But all of us have the chance to have a strong will. A heart that weighs in well.

It's up to each person to decide.

One of the nice things about running is that you only have to go one step at a time. I wouldn't think I could go six miles, if I had to think that far ahead.

I can't even envision a marathon.

Even the daily jog turns me off, if I look at the whole thing.

But I *can* think about taking another step. That I can decide, and somehow, by a miracle of repetition, I get the job done or the race run.

One step at a time.

I think it was some older guy with a guitar that sang a song about that: "I'm following Jesus, one step at a time."

One time when I was talking to a group of children about walking in Christ, I asked, "How many steps did the Apostle Paul take at a time when he walked?"

I could see their little minds working hard. Finally one dared to answer: "One!"

Very true. The most spiritual of giants still goes one step at a time.

"Yard by yard, it's hard.

"Inch by inch, it's a cinch."

Well, it isn't all that easy even in the short strides, but life *is* meant to be lived a step at a time.

When I run, several things are pretty obvious:

1. *I go only one direction.* No matter where I'm running to, I've got to go one direction at a time. I've set my mind. And, of course, if I'm involved in an actual race, my mind has been made up for me because the course is already laid out.

2. *My head is in charge.* It tells my feet what to do. My feet don't look back up at my head and yell, "I'm not going to do it." They simply obey.

Unless, of course, there is some kind of problem or nerve damage . . . some real hurt could keep that from happening. But when all is well, my feet do what my head tells them.

3. *I run one step at a time.* It may seem like a long way from here to patience, or from here to loving somebody I don't like very well. But I can go a step at a time. I can do the next best thing. Or should I say, the thing I should do next, that's best.

I may not have a perfect marriage, but I can be running toward that, one step at a time. Maybe the next thing I should do is ask forgiveness in a certain area or improve the way I address my wife when I get home, or be more generous with money.

I can take one step.

That's the way to run. That's the way to follow Christ.

One step at a time.

It is a significant occasion and great feeling is involved when you make a decision of dedication or turn your whole love life or checkbook over to the Lord. Great! That is indeed a huge leap.

But then you have to start following your commitment and obeying God's will in the Scriptures one step at a time. Nobody ever jumped to the whole conclusion!

Even Paul was willing to say, "Not that I have already arrived."

So when you run, run steady. Run straight. Run with

clear direction.

But run one step at a time. With Christ.

That means do what you know to do now. Know He will be with you.

Kids pray for God's will for the future, yet don't do that will on Saturday evening. One step at a time.

Parents pray about what house to buy, yet aren't praying or caring about what word to speak when they address each other. One step at a time.

Pastors ask for enlargement and vision and great accomplishments, yet may not be getting ready for Sunday or praying about this or that. One step at a time.

God, in His kindness, gives us things we can do. He does so much for us in grace and then He urges us to follow Christ by the power of willing hearts. Obeying today. Then tomorrow. Then the next day. One step at a time. One day at a time.

I think I can hear Red Harper with his guitar now . . .

I'm really not that good a runner.

I struggle to endure and to stretch.

There are many times that I would just as soon quit running or run the wrong course.

I can say that I know how to keep up regular exercise and disciplines and be ready for the real tests of running that come up rather frequently, and it's true.

But my mind works funny, and plays tricks on me, and there are times when I could easily choose to quit the race.

I haven't. And I won't. But I need to face that tendency.

It's the same with physical jogging too. I'm not that good of a runner physically either.

But I'm trying, and I'm enjoying it.

But there are times I would just as soon quit.

This book is because of those two struggles, and written to help me keep running.

I hope you'll run with me.

To the end.
The tape. The finish.
The really great human race is to run with Christ and for Christ and by Christ.
It's a good race. It's a struggle.
It's an endurance run.
I can do it one step at a time.

2

DON'T LOOK BACK

"Brothers, I do not consider myself yet to have taken hold of it. But one thing I do: forgetting what is behind and straining toward what is ahead, I press on toward the goal to win the prize for which God has called me heavenward in Christ Jesus."

(Phil. 3:13-14, NIV)

Time flies. It marches on—a parade without a purpose for some.

But quickly it goes.

Here we are past 1984, and it was not George Orwell's. It was God's. And I am very glad.

Paul was God's too—and he had learned God's beautiful secret of grace about the past: forget it!

The past is gone. You cannot put wind in a bottle. You cannot contain it.

We cannot sell cans of Pentecost, having the winds of the Spirit trapped for our strength.

Every day's worship is for each day.

Don't live in the past. Don't try to eat so much breakfast tomorrow you won't have to eat the whole next week.

Worship Sundays, and come together in the body. That is as scriptural as can be. But worship Mondays and Thursdays too.

God is the great I AM. Lord of the now. He deserves our praise today.

Back when the four-minute mile was thought to be a dream, two men from England raced their way into the hearts of the world by crashing that invisible but crucial barrier. Roger Bannister and John Landy then faced each other in what was called the "miracle mile," to see which of the two record-breakers was faster.

It was a Super Bowl-type day in the history of racing. And Landy would have won, but he turned to look back just yards from the tape, lost a step, and Dr. Bannister slipped by on the other side.

"Remember Mrs. Lot!"

That quote from Jesus (I inserted the Mrs. to identify her!), recorded in Luke 17:32, is as clear as anything He says. As concise.

Don't forget one of the most interesting and horrible events of history, when a lady who had just been given freedom from an awful city that was about to go up in fire and brimstone lost everything by disobeying the clear and simple order: "Don't look back."

She is salt now. Old salt.

Runners have to keep their minds on the race ahead. They can't become proud about where they are in the race or how fast they've run thus far. They can't gloat. There's no time for that. There are other runners and the finish line is still in the distance.

Don't look back.

That does not mean that in life we are not grateful or do not take pictures and show slides of the past. It does not mean that we do not have memorial services or give eulogies.

But it means that we don't live in the past or bring up things that God has forgiven, or live with self-righteousness that hinders our running for Christ.

Don't look back.

When I run in 10K races, this issue is not so important. When I look back there's not much to see. At least not too many people! But the runners at the front of the pack who are really fighting for first and second and primary places have to live by the rule. They can ruin their finishes at the end if they don't.

Evangelicals, people of the fundamentals—I'm one of them—are notorious for living in the past. Some are card-carrying believers, who made the decision to trust in Christ, but then rely on the decision instead of growing in love.

They look at conversion as, "I did it," instead of, "God has begun a work in me."

Good runners keep stretching ahead. They honestly don't believe that yesterday's practice will make them feel OK today. They really don't think that the prize they won last year will help in the race next year.

There are three things in our Christian lives that we

should not look back at because they weaken us.

1. *Don't look back at sin.* That's what I'm going to accuse Mrs. Lot of doing. She was to leave the city. Get out. Vacate.

Something like repentance, what she did was to be complete in the sense that she really meant it.

But remember how, on her way, she turned to take a last look at the city. There is no editorializing in the Scriptures about why she did it. Maybe there was a sale on downtown, and she needed one last look at the bargains. Maybe she simply had second thoughts about evacuating. Whatever the case, she "left her heart in San Francisco" as she disobeyed the orders of the Lord.

Nobody had a chance to interview her after this horrible episode. Lot and the rest of his family had to keep going.

Don't look back at sin. Don't pretend it didn't happen, but don't gloat about it or live in the past. Forgive yourself after you accept God's forgiveness. Forgive others.

We easily look back at our own sins and hold them against ourselves as if we're God. A chaplain at a Christian college told me recently that in his mushrooming counseling ministry so many of the cries were related to the past, and kids of twenty and twenty-one not being able to forgive themselves or to believe that their parents really loved them because of some things in the past.

Paul's letter to the Philippians was circulated in parts of Asia Minor where he had done his thing as an exterminator of Christians. Perhaps some who read Paul's "forgetting what lies behind" had remembered his ordering their parents to be killed or jailed for their faith. Maybe their believing children!

Now Paul could dare to say, "Forgetting what lies behind."

Apparently he believed God remembers our sins no more, as the Prophet Jeremiah rejoices (Jer. 31:34). He removes them from us as far as the east is from the west (Ps. 103:12).

And never the two shall meet.

I like that. It helps me sleep.

And run.

I am free and forgiven of my past because of Jesus Christ.

Those sins, confessed and forgiven, are—how did they used to say it?—under the blood.

I can't find them and should not try.

What do Moses, David, Peter, and Paul have in common, in addition to being among the best known of Bible people?

One common denominator: they forgot the past. They accepted grace for their miserable failures. They walked in the beauty of today. In God's grace.

Another consideration for spiritual runners who want to forget what's behind: don't hold grudges. That's looking back at the sins of others. Let them be. God has forgiven and the breach has been healed and anyone who looks back isn't being fair to the other runners or to himself.

Married couples live with frigid feelings or horrid lack of emotional joy because one of them can't forget what happened in '84 or seven years before. I knew a couple who did not say anything more intimate than "Pass the catsup" for sixteen years! They were punishing only themselves.

Don't look back at grudges and offenses from others.

Satchel Paige, the legendary major league pitcher who was a Yogi Berra-type philosopher, once said, "Don't look back—people might be gaining on you."

But our reasons to have a forward look while running are much higher.

A third consideration. Don't look back at sin in the sense of bringing up its fleshy feelings in your mind. It will only drive you backward as you seek to run forward. We are called to control our thought lives and not pretend we have no on-off switch.

Sometimes people do that in testimonies. You hear twenty minutes about the filth and the junk and then two minutes of how nice it is to accept Jesus.

I realize that sometimes you can't tell how good the doctor was until you understand the disease that was healed.

But I also think that there are some things which, when brought up, simply entice without edifying. Things too "shameful even to mention," as Paul put it once (Eph. 5:12, NIV).

Certainly balance is important, but let's make an effort to talk more about God's grace and less about the past.

I think it's healthy when Chuck Colson talks about the way he used to think and then what Christ did for him. Paul himself did that a bit.

But the emphasis was always on the beauty and rightness of Christ, and the now, and the future, and the power that makes it all possible!

"Go and sin no more," is something Jesus said to a woman caught in adultery.

Clearly she was to forget the past and cultivate some new habits. Clearly she was to leave yesterday behind. She was to get out while the getting was good.

But there are two other ways we can easily look backward as we run.

2. *Don't look back at self-righteousness.* That really is the whole context of Philippians 3 where Paul writes, "Forgetting those things which are behind" (v. 17, KJV).

What things?

All those titles and degrees listed in verses 5 and 6 of that same chapter, things which he once sincerely boasted in and relied on to get him "in" with God.

Clearly Paul was thinking of self-righteousness and standards that he had set up for himself, among them strict legalism.

"We are God's people, we are God's people," became a chant of some of the Israelis in the Old Testament as they rested on their past and sat down on their hindsight. Unfortunately, when you gloat about your past, you go nowhere in the present.

God wants us to live today with gratitude for the past and hope for the future—with love in our personal relationships. And with a heart warm toward Him. Now!

"Forgetting what lies behind . . . reaching forward to what lies ahead."

It's easy to be proud of the spiritual accomplishments of the past, bringing them up often to God or at least in our self-evaluations. But Christianity does not make rocking chairs out of trophies.

The man who is always glad that he did such good deacon work several years ago or that he taught Sunday School for seventeen years may be resting on his laurels instead of growing in God's grace.

One old hymn puts it this way: "I'm pressing on the upward way, new heights I'm gaining every day."

Don't make a scrapbook about your spiritual growth—make another step forward today!

Paul labels these laurels in no uncertain terms in Philippians 3:7. Are you ready for this? Dung!

Garbage.

Zilch.

Now he understands that a person is declared righteous not because of what he has done for God, but because he has received what God has done for him.

Quite a switch.

We call that a 180.

Paul wrote Romans to explain it in detail. There he presses down hard to show that all of us are unworthy in every way, and that we fall short of the finish line.

Way short.

But God sent His beloved Son, perfectly righteous, to pay the legal penalty for our sins and to share His own righteousness with all who would receive His gift.

And share it He does!

Imputeth is the word King James liked. God declares or judicially pronounces and gives—imputes—the righteousness of Jesus to me.

I am declared righteous because Christ's righteousness is covering me, not because I have done something swell.

This is justification.

This is what we are to stare at as we run.

Don't look back at or start repeating the erroneous way of living in your own "righteousness."

It really isn't all that right anyway.

It's more like filthy rags.

Paul's goodness and salvation were all wrapped in Jesus Christ. Look at Philippians 3:9, where he says that he wants to be found having Christ's righteousness now.

It's a whole different value system.

I love to read little children's letters to God, especially the one that was so succinct:

"Dear God,
Count me in.
Your friend,
Henry"

Henry had it together. He knew that whoever God counted in was going to make it.

So did Paul the Apostle.

God's system of righteousness is the one that matters. His way of reconciling us to Himself is the only one that works.

Running the race is not to get "in" with God. Let's be as clear on this as on anything.

People try all sorts of ways to gain God's favor, and their perceptions of grace are as distorted as their views of love.

But God brings us to Himself through His Son Jesus Christ and by the special grace that His Spirit endows. We decide and entrust ourselves to Him by believing in who He is and what He has done for us.

Salvation is a simple story about a Person who did some specific things to save us in a very complex way.

But it is simply received, by true faith.

That begins the running of the race.

If accepting Jesus Christ as Saviour is simple, so is the matter of spiritual growth. But because there are so many deviations and distractions on earth, it really becomes a complex issue.

It's like we're running the race and the course is clearly mapped out in most cases, but there are so many beautiful looking bypasses and so much hawking of cotton candy and extra attractions up in the stands. It's easy to get off the cinder path.

But we begin by faith, accepting Christ.

We continue by faith, accepting Christ.

Owning Him as Lord. Obeying Him as Master.

It is complex because we have so many drives, because of our fallen nature. It is complex because life has hard questions.

Someone has said that we have a shortage of simple problems and a surplus of simple answers.

True.

But righteousness as God has provided it for us *can* be talked about simply.

In a word: Jesus.

Don't look back at self-righteousness.

3. *Don't look back at secondaries.* Jesus could be awfully blunt at times. "Anyone who puts his hand to the plow and then keeps looking back is not fit for My kingdom," He

warned. "Don't go back home and bury your father or wait until he dies. Don't go investigate real estate opportunities. I have called you to follow Me!" (Luke 9:57ff, Larson paraphrase)

Clearly these people involved had been led by the Lord to become disciples. Clearly they knew what they were to do. Clearly they wanted to put other things in primary spots.

That does not mean that fathers should not be buried or real estate should not be scanned or appraised.

Don't feel guilty if you want to know whether you're going to stay in a motel or a home or a fox's hole when you go to another town.

The issue here is lordship. Jesus Christ should be obeyed whatever the cost. When you know what to do, you need to do it. I do too.

It's interesting to fly airlines which supply audio entertainment for their passengers. You put on your earphones and can choose country on channel 3 or comedy on channel 6 or rock on 7.

Similarly, all of us can choose to *what* we're going to listen or to *whom* in life. In a sense, we all get Solomon's choice of what we want to go after.

Don't look back at other issues but keep your eyes on Christ. That is the theme of Scripture.

There are so many, many sidelines today. It seems like half the world is here to invent things we could be majoring on instead of the will of our Lord.

Runners have many temptations. There are shade trees here and ice-cream stores there and cars that could take away the pain if ridden in! And there is nothing wrong with shade trees or ice-cream stores or automobiles!

In themselves.

But if you are in a race, they are not for you!

Don't turn to secondaries!

How many Christians are spending their energy and

money on things not wrong in themselves, but not the main issue?

"Follow Me," Jesus said.

"Don't look back."

"Don't go for the lesser."

"Love your God with all your might, and all your mind, and all your soul."

The opposite of looking back is looking at Jesus, and reaching forward to what lies ahead.

Paul said, "I press toward the mark." I pursue it. I strain toward it. I really want it.

"This one thing I do," he said.

David said, "One thing have I desired . . . that I may dwell in the house of the Lord . . . to behold the beauty of the Lord" (Ps. 27:4, KJV).

When Jesus complimented Mary for her interest in sitting at His feet to receive His truth, He said, "One thing is needful, and Mary has chosen that" (Luke 10:42, KJV).

Forgetting the past means concentrating on one main thing in life. "Whether, then, you eat or drink or whatever you do, do all to the glory of God," Paul said in another way (1 Cor. 10:31).

Some goals satisfy for an evening. Other passions can make you feel good for a summer. Some for a year.

But where is one that lasts?

Paul has found his, and it is good—to know Christ, and to press toward the mark of obeying Him!

Most of us Christians so easily live in the past, making nostalgia a lifestyle. Testimonies start with, "I remember the day I was saved."

Bravo.

If you asked me about how I'm living life and I said, "I remember the day I was born," you would try to get me to talk about the present.

It's so easy to live on yesterday's grace. Actually, not

yesterday's. Grace from twenty, thirty, forty years ago.

One recent testimony I heard went something like this: "I'm so glad I accepted Christ as my Saviour and I urge you to make that decision too. It was the greatest day of my life. And furthermore, I believe in the inspiration of Scripture."

Not much to say about how God has been working in his family or what good things have been happening or how he praises God for what happened a couple of days ago.

I think the date of submission to Jesus Christ as my Saviour may be a great help. I can't name the time and place, though I have memories of when and how.

But the big thing is that I do trust and that I am running in the present right now.

Wait—Paul said he was pressing toward the mark for the *future*, someone says. That's true. The future is to very much color our present. But if you read Philippians, you read about how to grapple with the now. The bitter now and now. The nasty now and now.

Of course, Paul did talk about how he sometimes wished he were home with the Lord, but he knew it was better to stay.

Forgetting the past.

That is an act of the will—a deliberate acceptance, one you are responsible for.

Do not run by it!

In a world of self-esteem themes and assertion books coming out our ears, it is very easy to stare into the mirror and forget our Lord.

"I press toward the mark," Paul said. God's call. God's mark. "The prize of the upward call of God in Christ Jesus," is the way Paul and the Holy Spirit put it (Phil. 3:14).

It is a rich phrase.

It covers heaven, our salvation, and the whole way of running to glorify God.

"Pressing on" is what the rest of this book is all about.

Pressing toward the mark for that gold, the prize.
Get on your mark . . .
Now don't look back . . .
Get set. . . .

3

RUNNERS ALREADY FINISHED

"Now faith is the assurance of things hoped for, the conviction of things not seen. For by it the men of old gained approval."

(Heb. 11:1-2)

"Therefore, since we have so great a cloud of witnesses surrounding us, let us also lay aside every encumbrance, and the sin which so easily entangles us, and let us run with endurance the race that is set before us."

(Heb. 12:1)

Some people picture the saints leaning out over the side of heaven and peeking down to watch us as we do our daily living. After all, they *are* called "witnesses."

Hebrews 12 begins with the great assertion, "Since we are surrounded by such a great cloud of witnesses" (v. 1, NIV).

The witnesses referred to here are the people of Hebrews 11. People who have been here before us and will witness to the fact that God is faithful.

They're not witnessing what we are doing right now, though that's debatable and people love to speculate. Instead, they give eternal testimony to the wonderful truth that God keeps His word.

Bring these witnesses to the stand, and you've got quite a list of knowns and unknowns, heroes and heroines, people who were made of flesh and blood but found strength from above in a very visible and special way.

Since we have witnesses like these, we know we can make it.

That kind of sentiment is all through the Bible. "You're not facing a test no one else has faced," Paul says in essence (1 Cor. 10:13). "Every test you face has been faced by others and Christ has gone through it too."

Paul and other writers are telling us that everyone is made of dust. Everyone has problems. Life is hard!

But others, many just like us, have come to the Lord for strength and found His reserve. They have obeyed His principles in Scripture and He has honored His promises.

We can do it too.

When I run in a race, I often meet runners who have already finished. I don't pass *them.* They pass *me* on their way back! It's rather frustrating to slowpokes like me when these men and women who have already finished get a few more miles or yards in at the end of the race and come back to greet us.

Where do they get all that stamina?

I'm huffing to make it to the end in the first place, and some of these guys look like they just had a bowl of Wheaties with Mary Lou Retton and now they are ready for a real race!

Actually, I'm thankful for a couple of them. Craig is a friend who often has finished, then come back to run the last mile or two with me. I always tell him as he runs alongside, "Tell me I can do it." He says, "You can do it." It helps.

"You're just saying that because I told you!"

"No, you can do it."

And because he has finished and is encouraging me, and because strength comes, I finish.

These people in Hebrews 11 are not flannelgraph people. They are people with normal testings, flesh, lusts, and pains. Their questions are just like ours. Should I cheat? Should I keep going? Will God stick with me in this painful event even though things look bleak?

Nothing's really changed.

When you read Hebrews 11, you come away knowing this about faith:

1. *It's the only way to please God.* He really does want to be believed. He wants us to think He is truth. According to Hebrews 11:6, "Without faith it is impossible to please Him, for he who comes to God must believe that He is, and that He is a rewarder of those who seek Him."

2. *Faith is not just a feeling, but a response to a revelation.* It "comes by hearing, and hearing by the Word of God" (Rom. 10:17, KJV).

One man told me recently, "I believe God. But I just don't know how to have faith."

"You've got it," I told him.

He was surprised. It was like he had just won a quiz show. I don't want to play with semantics here, but faith is a noun form of *believe*, and believing comes when we really take God at His Word. We say that we think it's true and act as if we do.

That's what the people in Hebrews 11 did.

3. *When we act on faith, God keeps the word of faith and the promises attached.* That's really what Hebrews 11 is about. It's to get you ready for the race spelled out in Hebrews 12–13. Those chapters are loaded with practical ideas about obeying the Lord. Everything from how to treat your pastor to how to treat your wife, from how to handle a bitter spirit to how to handle money. All kinds of things that have to do with the daily nitty-gritty.

But you're not going to be able to do that very well unless you really believe Hebrews 1–10 about justification. And then when you read Hebrews 11 you can see that others believed God and they seemed to flourish spiritually!

So keep running. John did. Charlie did. And so on. . . .

Let's hear from Mr. and Mrs. Abraham. That's Abraham and Sarah. As they walk up the aisle to the witness stand at ages 94 and 100, you'd see them smiling on the way. "We had no idea how God wanted to use us or what He really meant about our starting a family that would become a great nation. Sarah laughed, and our neighbors thought it was really unbelievable, but God kept His word. And then we had to pack our bags and leave home forever. We didn't know where God was leading us. I guess faith means you believe God knows best and you take Him at His word."

Bring Moses to the witness stand. "Moses, did you find God faithful to His word?"

"Boy, I had a tough choice. Some of me wanted to stay there in Pharaoh's court and become one of the inside men in Egypt. It was a pretty nice opportunity. But I really did want to believe God and I finally chose that. Am I ever glad. I'll tell you how He helped me. . . ."

There's a lot in Hebrews 11 about Israel and Moses the leader. But Israel really blew it, simply because they could not live by faith—even though God was doing miracles right in front of them! God was willing to go a day at a time with them, but they wanted to walk by sight. Israel didn't want manna enough for a day, but extra shelves full.

We often act the same way, expecting God to supply a week's worth of patience or a month's worth of joy. Faith doesn't work that way. Faith means you trust God a moment at a time and for each day, and you believe that even in the tests you're experiencing right now, He is there.

Bring Rahab up to the witness stand. Let's hear what a lady says.

"I really had messed up my life, and I knew it. Seemed like my reputation and my pigeonhole were set in cement. And then I believed something related to a scarlet cord and the promise of men representing God, and that faith was the key to a whole new way to live.

"I feel so clean! And I'll tell you, God is true to His word."

You need to hear more? The entire transcript is available in these forty verses. Read it and see what God did for those people. They "conquered kingdoms, performed acts of righteousness, obtained promises, shut the mouths of lions, quenched the power of fire, escaped the edge of the sword, from weakness were made strong, became mighty in war, put foreign armies to flight" (Heb. 11:33-34).

And that's just the beginning of it.

It's so easy to forget. I look back in my life and see the ways God has rescued me over and over again.

I am convinced that God's sovereignty and His protection have been upon me as much as the fire and cloud led Israel through the wilderness.

I don't mean in the sense of guidance, because I couldn't always see what He was saying so clearly. But when I look back, I know He has been in charge and has been my Shepherd.

There are more promises that the Lord will shepherd us than there are commands for us to follow Him. That doesn't prove anything in itself, but I do believe that when your heart is right, you can't make a mistake. He will shepherd and guide, and you will choose carefully and be used of Him to run this race for His glory.

Sometimes I've made choices on the basis of faith just because I knew the Word said it. And I felt good about it later, but not at the time. Just as often, I have struggled with my own lusts or feelings and barely made the right choice. But I took the next step.

I did not faint.

And that's one of God's promises too.

Sometimes we soar like the eagles, other times we run without tiring, and sometimes the best we can do is to take another feeble step.

But not faint.

See Isaiah 40:31. It's pretty clear.

Faith isn't always mountaintop stuff. It isn't always singing at the top of your voice.

Sometimes faith means you're simply willing to do what you know is right, despite your feelings. But you know you need to take that next step, and God helps you in that tough situation and somehow gives grace and strength in weakness.

And you do not quit. You keep running and working.

I remember when President John F. Kennedy initiated a national physical fitness kick to try to reduce the blubber and cholesterol content of modern Americans. (I think it was one of his most significant lighter accomplishments.)

He appointed Bud Wilkinson, the successful coach of college football's Oklahoma Sooners, as the chairman of the fitness campaign.

It was also the very time when professional football was becoming the new national religion, surging to the top of the charts almost overnight.

It was halftime at one of the nationally televised games, and Wilkinson was being interviewed by one of the network announcers who asked, "What has the rise in interest in pro football done to help President Kennedy's call for physical fitness?"

"Nothing."

The announcer thought that Wilkinson must not have heard the question correctly. He asked it again.

"Nothing," Wilkinson answered again.

And then came the coach's often-quoted insightful explanation: "Pro football is twenty-two tired men who desperately need rest being watched by millions of people who desperately need exercise."

And the proportions are something similar in evangelical churches. Many people who desperately need a rest or at least could use help are being watched and often criticized by all kinds of people who desperately need spiritual exercise.

And the more you get into the race of following Christ personally, the more you realize the need to be in shape spiritually.

If you just sit in a car and throw out the keys, you will not need to stop at a gas station. You're not even going to drive. Likewise, you don't need the ministry of the Word of God very much if you're not going to give it out to serve others.

Could that be why so many people become simply spectator-critics, Monday-morning quarterbacks who speak negatively of other ministers, but have no feeling of ministry fitness themselves?

Methinks so.

I don't think the Hebrews 11 people were always serving or always on top of it or always smiling inside and out. Let's call David to the witness stand.

"I know what some of you are thinking. I really blew it. I admit it. I mean I was as low as you could get. I thought it was all over between me and God. But I want to tell you how

He rescued me and created a clean heart within me and gave me a whole new life.

"I'm sorry for what I did, but I'm not sorry for how big His grace became to me. I can't tell you how amazing and constant is His love, even after the sinful things I did."

Some marathon runners were part of a survey in *Marathon* magazine once about what keeps them going in a race. Their answers:

1. The encouragement of other runners and people along the course
2. Fluids
3. Hope (the finish line)

When I see the lead runners coming back the other way, I know the finish line can't be too far off. I know that it is possible to make it to the end. And then when they, with added love, encourage me to make it and tell me I can, I *know* I can.

And I always feel so glad that I've finished.

Hebrews 11 winds up the list of witnesses by saying that God has "provided something better for us" (v. 40). Don't be afraid to call the New Testament better. The New Covenant is related to forgiveness that's total and redemption that's been so pictured at Calvary that there can be no question in our minds but what God has already judged our sin.

Sure it's better.

I'd much rather live under grace than under the faith plan of the Old Testament. I'd much rather live looking back at the Cross of Christ than looking ahead to it.

And as soon as I say that, I'm also saying that I should live in a better way. I should follow Christ in an even stronger way than those men and women of the Old Testament. They didn't have all the promises we have. They didn't have all the presentations of love and grace that God has given.

They had faith.

We can have both.

And when we do exercise faith, God will usually use us to help people who are experiencing the same difficulties in their own spiritual races. He always wants us to be "comforting those . . . with the comfort with which we are comforted" (2 Cor. 1:4).

Redundant? Maybe. Reassuring? Unquestionably! When you comfort people with the comfort with which you have been comforted, you are telling them how you made it and that they can make it too!

The runners of Hebrews 11 do that through the printed page. We can do it through personal contact and encouragement.

Not too long ago I went through a time of searching and wavering to make some of the most difficult decisions of my life, which involved leaving a church where my roots were deep and my love was strong. I went through a period of depression. First time in my life. I hope the last.

I lost about seventeen pounds over three or four months, a few friends who didn't understand what they perceived to be my indecision or even how I could possibly begin to leave, and quite a few nights of sleep and meals.

I would lie in the bed and look at the ceiling (my wife called it my cadaver pose) and wait for God to say a little more. But He was so very silent.

I waved my hanky, and He didn't say anything.

I asked for a lightning bolt or at least a lightning bug that would show me what to do.

During that time, one special friend kept telling me, "You can't make a mistake."

He had faced a similar decision about pulling up roots not too many years before. Yet he didn't just throw his situation at me and say, "I did it and you can do it too." Instead, he was truly empathetic.

I also called a friend, an author-psychologist whose name you would know, and asked him if my fears or my feelings were inappropriate. He said that he was still going through depression over a move he had made in his life a few years before! And then he laughed.

The statement didn't help, but the laugh did.

Since you're interested, I should tell you that the end of this story is very special. I made a choice, my family concurred, and the things that we looked for as open doors all swung open. Miraculously, the depression lifted as I drove from my fifteen-year assignment to the new one. On the very day that I made the trip, it was like a cloud was leaking out of my chest and evaporating through the side window of the car as we drove.

My fear that I would begin the new ministry as the great depressed leader vanished and joy returned.

I don't know how to trace all those events or how much was mental and spiritual or anything like that.

I just know how to thank God.

And I know that the light at the end of the tunnel could be another train coming or just New Jersey, but I also know that God can get me through it.

He did it in Hebrews 11. He did it in my life. He's done it for so many.

He'll do it for you.

Keep running!

I don't know how to finish a race except one step at a time.

I realize you project yourself toward the end and you start thinking about the finish line and how nice it's going to be to grab a hunk of orange or a drink of water again, but you still have to lean up and take one more step.

Lots of runners urge you when you're going up a hill not to look at the top but to look down at the road and just let the whole thing happen and soon you're at the top.

Maybe so.

My friend had told me, "Lean down, and take shorter steps" when he rescued me running up that big hill in my first race.

Learn humility, and just go a step at a time. Not a big step. Just make the decision that will help you through today.

Forgive that person. Love your wife, honor your husband. Talk to the Lord. Keep your ethics straight.

He'll guide you. He said He would shepherd you "for His name's sake," so He's got a lot invested in this.

His reputation.

You can do it.

Others have!

"Since we have so great a cloud of witnesses . . . let us run with endurance the race that is set before us."

4

RUNNING WITH SPEED, WITHOUT WEIGHTS

"Therefore, since we have so great a cloud of witnesses surrounding us, let us also lay aside every encumbrance, and the sin which so easily entangles us, and let us run with endurance the race that is set before us, fixing our eyes on Jesus, the author and perfecter of faith, who for the joy set before Him endured the cross, despising the shame, and has sat down at the right hand of the throne of God. For consider Him who has endured such hostility by sinners against Himself, so that you may not grow weary and lose heart."

(Heb. 12:1-3)

Carbohydrate loading goes something like this. About a week before the race, you run all-out. Maybe ninety minutes if you can do it. I'm talking about serious runners and getting ready for serious runs.

Then for three days you skip all carbohydrates and go with meat and fish, cheese and eggs. You continue training.

Then for the last three days you stop training and go with pasta and other foods high in carbohydrates.

Some experiments show that by following such a regimen you increase your power for the race one to three times.

No wonder many serious runners are becoming loaders.

I don't think any exact parallel to carbohydrate loading exists in Christianity. You don't load up on Scripture for three days and then stay off of it. But I do think we go through cycles, and that we need certain times of special prayer.

We become guilty that Martin Luther prayed two hours every day because he had a busy day ahead, and we don't do the same thing. So we decide not to pray for two minutes. And then we get guilty because we haven't talked to God, so we don't talk to Him because we feel guilty. I have lived in this cycle, though I try to refuse it. He knows me. He knows me like a book. And a little better.

And He knows that in my weakness I can turn to His strength. He knows when His son (me, that is) comes home again to enjoy His grace. He knows that I need His Scripture and that I'm sorry I skipped yesterday.

So I can run today. That's the nice part spiritually—the cycles can be broken and yet He brings me back.

But I do need discipline. I need regularity. I need Sunday worship, but worship on a regular basis during the week too.

I need to bring up Christianity in conversations or it never gets brought up.

I need to talk about Christ with a new friend or I'll be

embarrassed a year later.

Regimens are as necessary for spiritual "athletes" as for physical ones. These habits will differ for all of us, so we must find those best for us and then do them.

Part of this goal is to erase "encumbrances," the things that hold us back.

It's like the drama at the beginning of a race. In a sprint, six to eight runners are out there taking off their sweat suits. Even in chilly spring weather, they strip to the bare minimum. Track shoes are so light and dainty now that it's hard to believe they can be so sturdy.

Wait a minute! There's another runner getting ready. He's got a three-piece suit and a white button-down shirt and tie. He wants to go the distance too.

The crowd smiles. Runners run without such weights or they don't do too well!

So it is in Hebrews 12.

"Let us lay aside every weight, and the sin which does so easily beset us, and let us run with patience the race that is set before us" (Heb. 12:1, KJV).

I wonder if those weights (*encumbrances* in the *New American Standard Bible*) are perhaps the things we add to our lives that aren't necessarily sins, but just aren't God's best for us.

We all know the feeling of having to choose between the better and the best at times.

Good runners lay aside weights. They strip away the nonessentials.

And that's what we're committed to be: good runners.

One of the weights is legalism. That's a sin, though we don't like to call it that. In my mind, legalism is just as bad as modernism. Probably just as prevalent.

It's a weight. This keeping-the-Law stuff to stay in God's love, or picturing His love as so conditional that if we don't agree with another man about how long our hair should be or how to spend Sunday or even how to vote, that we're in trouble . . . all of that weighs us down.

Unbelievers watch us run and can't believe how slow we are in some things.

Slow to love.

Slow to rejoice.

Slow to give thanks.

No wonder some people don't choose the race we're in.

Lay aside those weights, the writer to the Hebrews says. It's the only way you're going to run with any degree of success.

A man came to a police station terribly upset. His apartment smelled so bad he couldn't stand it.

"It's my two brothers' fault," he complained. "One keeps pet turtles and the other has goldfish. The place is a mess. It stinks. Aren't there laws?"

"No," replied the officer, trying to calm the man down. Then he asked, "Why don't you just open the windows and get rid of the odor that way?"

"And lose all my pigeons?" the man exclaimed.

It *is* hard to see our own faults. It's hard to really notice those weights that are keeping us back. A grudge against someone, a habit of too much TV that keeps us from the Word and family communication, a love for food that's beyond the bounds of good taste—all easily go unnoticed. Even the desire to work too hard or to prove something when God has already accepted us can hold us back spiritually.

A three-piece suit is fine for certain occasions, but hardly appropriate for a footrace.

I know that. But if I look in the mirror and forget the race, I might just think about how nice the suit looks. Instead, I need to consider what I'm really about, and why I'm running, and if the suit relates to that goal in a good way.

I'm convinced that TV has influenced us in three major areas, two of which are attacked all the time: sex and violence. You can't watch television without getting a little more familiar with both and getting those lust motors revving in your body.

But a third effect is just as bad and maybe a bit more subtle—the area of passivity. Television has made spectators of us all, to the point that family communication and activities are becoming endangered species. Not to mention spiritual growth.

You would think a runner who has his overcoat on would realize it pretty quickly once the race begins. He usually does. But in this thing called spiritual or Christian living, it's so easy to not see how a habit holds us back.

Personally, I think it's great that churches have distinctives. Everybody has to find what he believes and stick with it.

But if my distinctive or the things I like at church become one and the same with the message of the Gospel, then I've just added a weight to the Gospel.

I don't think that God wants us telling people who swear ten reasons why they shouldn't swear, if their real problem is that they don't even believe in Jesus Christ.

Unbelievers often find Christianity too heavy. They can't see the forest for the trees we place in their way.

Grace is not heavy.

Oh, theologically it is, and the background of it is so tremendous and God has done so much.

But Jesus called men to Himself because His "burden is light."

So why do we beef up the Gospel message with our own ideas or add a bit of WASP influence or conservative Republican ideas and then hope somebody will trust Jesus?

Mark Hatfield's a Christian too!

I hope our church will always be big enough to have Mark Hatfield and Jesse Helms as members at the same time.

Maybe they could even serve on the same committee.

Certainly I'm not suggesting that we live without rules. I just think that in areas of doctrinal insignificance, we should remember that rules are individual, not universal. In other words, keep them to yourself, but don't expect them of others.

Be hard on yourself, but easy on others.

Sure, I have disciplines about entertainment and things I eat and what I do on Sunday. But I can't impose my standards on others.

Sure, I turn off the TV at certain times and try to restrict my viewing hours, but I can't expect the same standard for everyone else, or think it keeps me in with God.

Lay aside the weights.

Be able to distinguish the difference between scriptural commands and personal customs and obligations.

It's not as easy as it sounds. The insurance salesman must invest upwards of sixty hours a week to attract new clients. A restaurant manager is almost owned by the chain. A homemaker can be so involved cooking, cleaning, and caring for the children that she has little time for herself, let alone God.

Yes, to get good at running after Christ, and laying aside weights, is not so very easy.

But necessary.

That's where choices come in, and the daily discipline.

One of the best gifts God ever gave us was choice. The ability to decide what we're going to do. In fact, God calls us to choose. It's mandatory. Choice makes us try to think through what will speed us up and what will hold us back.

One time I ran in a five-mile race where it was simply out and back. That's the kind of race that increases embarrassment because you see exactly where you are in the whole picture, as all those frontrunners pass you on their return trips.

That day it was chilly enough that I kept some longer cotton running pants on over my shorts, and a running sweatshirt over my T-shirt.

And then the rain came.

My pants got soaked and heavy. The sweatshirt too.

On my way back I finally had enough sense to stop and take those garments off and hand them to one of the mile-marker people who would bring them in later.

It was bad enough that I was going to finish 200th out of 270! The wet sweats would drop me back further!

They tell about the frog that swallowed one BB at a time until it had so many inside, it couldn't get up. Or the other frog—why is it always frogs?—that jumped in hot water and jumped right back out, and another that jumped in lukewarm water and got boiled to death because it didn't notice the rising temperature.

Weights work that way. They take over our lives or become our obsession without our knowing it. Even social-action issues become the center of our attention so easily, instead of Christ.

Yes, the world needs to stop abortion. Yes, we need guardianship of our neighborhoods against pornography, given the statistics we now see that relate it to such horrible crimes and misuse of families and bodies.

Yes, Christians need to be in public office, and public officers need to be ethical and righteous as best they can.

But the world needs Christ before all of that or on top of all of that.

Let's not argue about the order of all this, but let's be sure that the main message and the main goal of life is first related to obedience to Christ and being His people in the world, and that the message we share about accepting Christ is one that's very clear about grace and not what *we* do for Him.

Those weights can be shaken, but it's hard.

I remember the first time I went into a theater after growing up under a Sunday School teacher—someone very special to me—who warned that if I went into a movie house and Jesus Christ returned to the world I would not go along with Him in the Rapture.

I remember coming out of the theater with more fear than that which I had just experienced minutes before watching King Kong do his thing in New York City. I was scared to death I would see cars wrecked here and there and realize that suddenly the Rapture had come and I'd been left behind.

Isn't there a song like that?

There's another song that talks about "marvelous, infinite, matchless grace."

And another one that says, "Saved by grace alone, this is all my plea. Jesus died for all mankind, and Jesus died for me."

James Montgomery Boice talks about the man who thought that song said, "Jesus died for old man Kline," instead of "all mankind."

But it's true.

Jesus died for Knute Larson.

Jesus died for you.

And that grace message, while it lays some heavy implications and obligations on us, is first a beautiful, clear, and simple story about a Man who came into a world with a message of trust and who died for us on the cross.

Let's get rid of the weights and run with endurance. Share the story with simplicity. Live the life with obvious obedience.

One of the things that concentrating on weights and your personal spiritual growth does is to get you in touch with who you are. People who simply are going through life without paying attention to the encumbrances or the Spirit are letting their bodies run away with them in a sense.

Maybe that's an exaggeration.

But I know that when I grapple with my will, and face head-on God's commands about being unselfish or keeping the Golden Rule or witnessing, I grapple with the stuff I'm really made of. When I see something lying on the floor, I know that if my wife were around she'd really like to have it picked up. Though it doesn't really matter to me, the Golden Rule says that I should put the dirty socks in the hamper because it would be doing something nice for my wife. And because I like people to do nice things for me—are you still with me?—I take a hard look at who I am. I'm not just letting my body feed me pizza or take me to bed again.

I'm grappling with some of the hard facts of life. At the moment I may not care about the Golden Rule. I don't care if my wife would like me to do something helpful for her.

Unfortunately, "I don't care" can become a way of life.

But the Christian is called to a whole life of caring and to a whole different way of living. To a life that is running. Running the race with Christ. It's not a paranoia or a neurosis or a constant introspection, but it *is* grappling with the real you.

Let's face it. Running itself can become a weight. You can get so obsessed with running or any other physical activity that you neglect things that are more important. Brains and brawn and bosoms are in right now, and it's so easy to spend more hours taking care of your body than you do your soul.

It's easy to make Paul's words to Timothy, "Bodily exercise is all right . . . " your life verse.

Read further, though, for Paul also says, "But spiritual exercise is much more important and is a tonic for all you do" (1 Tim. 4:8, TLB).

Again, weights come easily.

I believe weights are put there to help us work out. They help us figure out where we're going and what we really want and why it's really best.

They get us to center on what needs to be centered on!

If we didn't have to grapple with where we should live or what kind of vocation we should have or whether we should be married and, if so, to whom, and where we should go to school or how we should spend our evenings—if all those things were presto notes dropped down from heaven, little memos written by God Himself, we'd never have to think or work out or stretch or choose or seek wisdom.

We wouldn't be running anywhere.

We would be puppets, strung on strings and responding as God says.

But instead we have to deal with getting rid of weights and handling things that seem OK at first, but then hold us back. We must grapple with criticisms from others and look for the kernel of truth and what we should do about it and when.

So, the questions of life and the hard struggles of running are good for us.

The runner who is thirty pounds overweight and wants to prep for a race has got some discipline to go, but he's got a great victory celebration ahead as he loses the weight and feels better and makes the run and finishes the course!

The fact is that he probably doesn't have a victory celebration as much as he has a progress celebration because he's going to have to watch his weight regularly in the years ahead.

So it never really ends.

The laying aside of weights really becomes a constant, as we make daily decisions about what's best and what keeps us on course.

"Choose ye this day," is probably just as appropriate as "Choose you for the rest of your life."

Surely there are choices that determine our destiny and that relate to accepting Christ or dedicating our bodies, but every day there are other choices that make us cleaner or that keep us running in a better way.

Laying aside every weight . . .

Some people run physically because they think it prolongs their lives. I'm not sure you can do that. Maybe you can die with a seventy-eight-year-old body but the cardiovascular system of a twenty-eight-year-old.

Maybe you're more comfortable as you go.

I don't mean to be irreverent about death, but I'm not sure that you can actually prolong your days. I do know you can shorten them. Solomon writes, "Do not be a fool. Why should you die before your time?" (Ecc. 7:17)

If a fatalistic fanatic stands at the railroad tracks and says that the choo-choo train won't kill him unless it's his time, I say it's his time. Or at least, as a fool, he has died before his time.

Yes, physical running can add something special to your life.

But here's the great parallel and the one where I clap for joy. Spiritual running *does* prolong your life. It gives you eternity!

Not a bad reason to run for Christ. Not a bad reason to accept Christ as Saviour and Lord and rejoice in His grace.

"He who has the Son has life," John says (1 John 5:12, NIV). The opposite is death, and everyone has that going for him already. In a sense, we are all born dead, spiritually disconnected from God and therefore in need of revitalization. We need to get life.

That life comes with a plan from God Himself, which we don't even quite understand or always feel. It is a plan called salvation or redemption, and it produces life. It connects us with God through His Son Jesus Christ, who becomes our attorney or our go-between.

Nothing is more certain in Scripture than that the person who lives in Christ, or runs the Christian race, or trusts

Christ—however you want to put it, and the Scriptures put it many different ways—has eternal life.

Because he has Jesus Christ, the source of life.

He has the Son.

So run in Christ because there is life. Life more abundantly. Quality and quantity life.

A student said to Rollo May, "I know only two things—one, I will be dead someday; two, I am not dead now. The only question is what I shall do between those two points."

Well, you may wish to argue with what a man can know. You may wish to bring in the fact that he's going to pay taxes!

But the question remains vitally important—the question about what we shall do between the present and when God calls us home. That we can choose. That we can consciously will to do.

In short, we accept accountability. We learn where the best of life is. We choose it.

We lay aside weights.

We are glad.

5

"MINE'S GOSSIP— WHAT'S YOURS?"

"Therefore, since we have so great a cloud of witnesses surrounding us, let us also lay aside every encumbrance, and the sin which so easily entangles us, and let us run with endurance the race that is set before us, fixing our eyes on Jesus, the author and perfecter of faith, who for the joy set before Him endured the cross, despising the shame, and has sat down at the right hand of the throne of God."
(Heb. 12:1-2)

"See to it that no one comes short of the grace of God; that no root of bitterness springing up causes trouble, and by it many be defiled; that there be no immoral or godless person like Esau, who sold his own birthright for a single meal."
(Heb. 2:15-16)

All of us are failures—no question about that. We have all fallen short. Yes, some are shorter than others, if we must talk about it that way.

But that should give us no glee.

We are all in trouble.

Our daughter got a birthday card, from her cousin, whose cover read: "We got you this birthday card at a fraction of the original cost because it had a slight flaw in it."

And then you open it up.

Inside: "Merry Christmas."

A slight flaw, indeed!

We humans are in the same category.

We have nothing good in us. We are selfish.

You can go into one of those endless debates over how depraved the depravity is that we possess, or how far we fell, or what part of the image of God we lost, if any.

But the Scripture instead says we have sinned, that we do not seek God, that we are each saying, "Merry Christmas," when we ought to be wishing happy birthday.

Enter the Saviour.

The whole point of grace and of salvation is that God sent His Son to rescue us when we could do absolutely nothing for ourselves.

That's why I like the race. It gets me into eternal things.

But even with Christ in my life, I sin. And I suspect I understand that better all the time, so I remember to abide in my strength, Jesus Christ.

Otherwise I slide back to my weak points.

My besetting sins.

Besetting sins. The kind that you really enjoy.

This chapter will get pretty personal. You don't have to go any further if you don't wish.

The writer to the Hebrews tells us to lay aside every weight, and more: "the sin which does so easily beset [you]" (Heb. 12:1, KJV).

If you're going to run the race successfully, you have to get rid of the bulk that holds you back, the sin that keeps you down.

Sin messes up runners.

It's worse than shin splints.

Sin knocks the wind out of you, maybe not theologically, but personally.

If you don't get rid of the sins that beset you so easily, you soon find that you are hardly running at all.

You name the person, the friend, the deacon at church . . . the story of someone who for a while ran so carefully, looking unto Jesus, forgetting what was behind, reaching toward the mark . . . even buffeting his body.

But then somehow he let sin, in whatever form, take over a closet and then a corner, a room, and then a floor.

In Hebrews 12, it's my opinion that the sin could easily be that of unbelief. The context is believing the Lord. Hebrews 1–10 is especially about believing Him for righteousness and for the New Covenant.

Hebrews 11 is about people who did that, who took God at His word.

Now, if we're going to run and take Him at His word, if we're going to make progress in our lives, we can't carry the load of sin.

We've got to believe God.

Believing God is not all that easy. He talks in language we sometimes don't comprehend. He's always talking about righteousness and holiness and humility and loving others, and we're always talking about ourselves.

God is always talking about things that last for eternity, and we're always on an urgent dash for something in the present.

"Now" is our middle name.

Faith is when we believe God and take Him at His word, having heard what He says in Scripture.

Faith is doing what God says we should do, not through an earphone, but through the written Word of God.

Conversely, the sin of unbelief is going by what we feel instead of what we read and believe.

According to the Apostle Paul in Galatians 5:16-23, we should choose to walk in the Spirit; only then will we not carry out the feelings of the flesh.

The feelings of the flesh are just plain constant. They are those thoughts we think whenever we make a mistake. Notice how some excuse pops into your mind to blame someone else. That's a feeling of the flesh. So too are thoughts that come when we stare the wrong way or want revenge.

Instead, we're to choose to go by faith. To do what the Scriptures say.

That is a walk. A run, if you please.

A step at a time, in the Spirit of Christ, according to His written Word.

The only way anyone's going to live without the besetting sin of "unfaith" or unbelief is to know the Word and then proceed to do it. Where it is clear, be clear. Where it is hazy, be careful.

"We walk by faith, not by sight," Paul says (2 Cor. 5:7).

That is, of course, not easy. We would rather see the outcome.

The Bible talks about "the gift of faith" (1 Cor. 12:9), and I know some people who may have it. I don't.

I find it difficult to pray for something and get up from my knees and believe it's really going to happen. Yet, I have met others who have such George Mueller-type faith when they pray that it sometimes embarrasses me.

Sometimes I am embarrassed because I know they can't possibly be right, and they represent Christians like me.

Sometimes I am embarrassed because I wish I could believe like they do, especially when I see their prayers come true.

So I have to work at faith, if that's not a mixed metaphor. Where God is clear, that's one thing. But to stretch my faith and share that vision with my church takes the hard work of belief for me.

I can really sympathize with people like Abraham and Moses and the other saints listed in Hebrews 11, and the tensions they must have felt when God told them to do something that seemed so impossible and even invisible! I probably would have called for a committee to study the meaning of God's words to be sure that we were understanding them right.

To believe God does not rule out questioning Him, but it does get us on the right spiritual road.

We have it so much easier than most of the people in Hebrews 11 in that we have the Scriptures in black and white. Often they heard a voice or had a dream or got clear directions from God, but nobody else could see where they got it. That had to be something.

Stretching, to say the least!

But when they did it, and went after what God was holding in front of them, their rewards were very special.

Look what Abraham and Moses have done for the world, for instance!

They were willing to live for the eternal, and, in some cases, to skip parts of now.

That's difficult.

Faith looks beyond today and believes that obedience to God makes for a better tomorrow.

Faith takes God at His word.

Faith is a conviction that must sometimes beat down feelings and keep us on the right path.

Lack of faith besets us!

Overcoming your besetting sin may mean really believing God when you pray, believing that His way is right when you feel otherwise. Believing that it's correct to love others instead of getting even or spreading gossip.

Gossip or revenge may seem therapeutic, but those feelings are deceiving.

What God says is healthiest for us is best in the long run.

And that's the kind of run He is interested in.

But there's more. It could be that each one of us must also grapple with our own besetting sins. From a practical standpoint, even if that's not the main interpretation of Hebrews 12:1, all of us admit that certain sins bother us more than others.

I personally have never had a problem stealing or thinking about it. Like "Honest Abe" Lincoln, I'd return extra change at the store if the clerk mistakenly gave it to me.

And if I stop there, I'll get real proud!

But there *are* sins I grapple with constantly. I was laughing with a group of friends about telling our favorite sin or the one that besets us more than others. "Quick, Don," I said to a friend, "tell me yours. Mine's gossip, and I'd like to share yours!"

Not true, but I have some friends whose favorite sin is gossip. Former friends.

No, I haven't grappled with stealing and I'd like to think I stay pretty clean in the area of gossip, but selfishness related to pride of achievement or looking at another person the wrong way is a sin I constantly struggle with. I have to lay aside that sin that so easily besets me or I'll never run straight.

I can only do that with the help of Christ. I can only do that as I honestly confess sin and ask for His strength in my weakness.

Maybe besetting sins come from genes or heredity. Maybe there is more that's right in Freud than we want to admit about bent toward certain sins. Maybe it's just that everybody faces selfishness and pride and lust of the flesh, but doesn't talk about it much.

I don't know for sure. But I know that if I don't keep my mind on Christ and look toward Him, the besetting sin can dominate.

A nationally known speaker and I were sitting together at a banquet where he was speaking and I was emceeing, and he took time for a question-answer session from the seminary students attending the banquet. The first question he was asked, in this large, mixed, moldable audience: "Pastor, what would you say is the sin that tempts you more than any other?"

It got pretty quiet. I was curious to see how he would handle this.

People were taking notes.

His answer: "Well, aside from the normal sins of the lust of the flesh and the lust of the eyes and the pride of life, I would say that I especially have to grapple with the area of impatience."

Quite an answer.

When he sat down I leaned over and whispered, "You covered quite a mouthful with that first sentence."

He smiled.

The Apostle John knew. Inspired by God, he labels those lusts so threatening to every believer running the race. He tells us that we are not to love the world, and that the lusts of the world will forever be trying to sneak into the cracks and crevices (1 John 2:16). Besetting sins.

What's yours?

What are you doing to combat it?

Certain defenses need to be built in. And certainly we all need to learn to walk in the Spirit.

The besetting sin of temper may come with red hair or a short fuse that was inherited from Dad or Mom.

The besetting sin of not knowing how to reach out and love may come from a family where there was so much quietness at home that no one ever learned to communicate.

The besetting sin of lust may come because of lack of affection or self-worth that is always reaching out in the wrong ways.

The besetting sin of lying may be a habit learned in third grade that never was confronted or broken.

It's there. You know it. You look in the mirror and could easily identify it, even if it doesn't show.

The late Vance Havner always used to tell the story of the man who went up front at a local revival meeting to repent and rededicate his life. Everyone seemed to be doing it.

A counselor friend was kneeling with this man at the front pew and urging him to confess his sins as a start to this time of spiritual renewal.

The man said that he couldn't think of any of his sins. His friend countered with, "Guess at them!"

And as Vance Havner used to say: "He guessed them right the first time."

If you can't think of sins that bother you regularly, just guess at them.

Probably you'll guess them right.

Or at least you won't be far off.

One thing is true—we're all made of flesh. "Prone to wander, Lord, I feel it—prone to leave the God I love," the old hymn, "Come, Thou Fount of Every Blessing," puts it.

And all of us would admit that. We are frail children of dust.

That same hymn also offers the solution: "Here's my heart, oh, take and seal it, seal it for Thy courts above."

Until we start singing that kind of rescue cry, and looking to God on a daily basis, we will stay with our besetting sins and even enjoy them.

Accepting Jesus Christ as Saviour has certainly never meant that anyone got rid of sin. We get rid of the penalty and now we have help to fight sin, but the choosing remains.

And some have allowed the sin's choices to come out first.

Pride, of course, is a besetting sin that stalks us all. It's always there, ready to bare its fangs and tentacles.

Pride produces lust and selfishness and materialistic desires.

Uncle Sam used to say, "Uncle Sam wants you," and that beckoning finger which pointed out from the poster to every American young man persuaded many of them to serve their country as soldiers.

Now the U.S. Army beckons, "Be all that you can be."

A different approach.

Now they must appeal to the same people who hear things like, "Have it your way," "You only go around once in life," and "Go for the gusto" day in and day out. Those Madison Avenue types know where the readers and listeners are.

They are into self. They're into sand castles.

They're into building extra closets because the present ones are full.

Or is it fool?

We so easily get comfortable with sins. We accept a fall over and over again and soon it becomes a part of our personality, a daily companion.

A runner of footraces has to work on areas that beset his performance.

For example, some runners who are hampered by shin splints must submit to a certain therapy to deal with that painful ailment and thus avoid it in the future. They can't just wait until healing occurs and then go out and run again. They must learn certain ways to lean while they run.

My friend, Conrad, can show you nine different exercises for nine different runners' ailments. You lay on your belly for this and on your side for that and stretch like a scissors with your legs for this one . . . and all of these prepare you for running but also correct a besetting ailment.

And then you're able to keep at it. To run with endurance. To finish the race. That goes for the spiritual run too.

But sin blinds and stumbles and ruins fellowship with our Lord.

Sin gets you doing so much less than God wants you to do.

Sin conquers—ultimately. It sneaks in and floods a little and then a little more.

Vince Lombardi was the great football coach of the Green Bay Packers in their prime. Once, the story is told, Leroy Caffey was loafing on a play in a practice session. "Caffey," said Lombardi, "if you cheat in practice, you will cheat in a game."

And Lombardi did not stop there. "And if you cheat in a game, you will cheat for the rest of your life. And I will not have it."

My friends, Carl and Jim, and I went out for track in high school. Carl put the shot. Jim threw javelin. I went out just to get in shape for football that fall.

The first week or so of practice consisted mostly of running three or four miles to build stamina. The three of us cheated. While others ran the whole way to Derry Street and back up Hale, we crossed over an alley and sat down beside some garbage cans near Hale to wait until everyone got back. Then we would break into the ranks—not at the very front of course; one doesn't want to cheat too obviously!—and impress the coach back at the stadium.

I finished with a strong sprint each time, and Coach "Zip" Thomas was duly impressed.

So impressed, in fact, that he put me down for the 100- and 200-yard dashes at the first meet, against York High.

The day before, I could hear my friends (and others) laughing as they looked at the posting for Saturday's events.

Carl was down for shot put, and he did all right. Jim threw the javelin without embarrassment.

My races were something else.

I had to run against York's Johnny Mirtz, the Pennsylvania state champion in both dashes the year before.

Lee McFarlin and Jim Long were the other two runners for us, the great John Harris High School Pioneers.

I was nervous as we got set. With good reason.

Many of my friends (and others) had come out to see this great human race.

The 100-yard dash was first. Bang! We're off! (They're off, then me.)

Johnny was great. He would be state champ again that year, and it showed.

Then Lee and Jim, two very swift guys.

Then the other two from York.

Then . . . after a pause, yours truly.

The fans went wild.

I went slowly.

The 200-yard dash was a repeat performance, except that the pause before my personal finish was longer.

The fans went wild again.

It would be my last sprint race.

Whom did I cheat? Who lost?

Whom do I hurt when I sin? Who loses?

If you cheat in practice, why not in studies? If you cheat on your wife, why not cheat on your company? If you cheat on your company, why not on your wife? If you cheat on your personal income tax, why not with the corporate funds? If the President is immoral in the White House bedroom, why not in the Oval Office? God calls us to be clean and to be disciplined in all areas of life, even the smaller ones. Because all of life is for His glory.

"Whether, then, you eat or drink or whatever you do, do all to the glory of God" (1 Cor. 10:31).

It all matters.

A runner knows that both his food and his sleep the *days before* the race matter a lot on the *day of* the race. Some of them load up on spaghetti for days at a time, and then run the marathon. (I tried that once, but thought it just meant loading up the night before. So I ate a pile of linguine with great tomato sauce the night before, and I was fairly bloated. Only after the fact did I read that you load up on these carbohydrates starting about *a week* ahead.)

Willie Davis, one of the great Green Bay Packers, said of Vince Lombardi in a eulogy at his funeral, "All the man there is."

Wow! Who out there would be all the Christian there is? All the believer there is?

We make it so mystical, so mysterious, so miraculous.

Instead, it's a matter of worship and service and loving God and loving people, and I can do that if I wish, by the grace of Christ. When I will to do what's right, and walk in His Spirit, I don't have to worry about results. I simply am called to walk that day in His way.

All the man there is.

All the Christian there is. All the person that God means me to be.

Hebrews 12 is a chapter of victory, of going on to the end. It also talks about weak knees and bitter spirits. But first, it deals with the big issue:

1. Looking to Christ in a positive way.

2. As a part of that, getting rid of all that's negative—in other words, the sin—in our lives.

The daily call is to walk in the Spirit. For the context of this book, I might want to say, run in the Spirit.

But God seems to be emphasizing the one-step-at-a-time daily routine faithfulness.

There are four commands written to Christians about the Holy Spirit. Only four.

Of course, the Holy Spirit does many other things for us, but they are accomplished at the point of salvation, without our consciously seeking them. For example, when we place faith in Jesus Christ, we are born into God's family or regenerated by the Spirit (John 3:3-5; Rom. 8:9). We are baptized in, with, or by the Spirit (1 Cor. 12:13). By Christ's authority and action, we are sealed by the Spirit (2 Cor. 1:22; Eph. 1:13), are given spiritual gifts for ministry (1 Cor. 12:1-11), are indwelled by the Spirit (1 Cor. 6:19), and are anointed by the Spirit! (2 Cor. 1:21)

Back to the four clear commands.

1. "*Do not quench the Spirit*" (1 Thes. 5:19).

Don't throw a wet blanket on the fire of His love and leadership. In other words:

DESIRE HIS CONTROL.

This important command to Christians urges us to seek His leadership. Desire to be led by the Holy Spirit.

Want it more than anything else.

Jesus called it hungering and thirsting after righteousness (Matt. 5:6).

For an athlete to be in excellent condition, to be where he needs to be physically, he must follow a rigid program. But even before that, he must make the choice, and desire that goal.

Otherwise he will give up too soon.

Desire the control of the Spirit.

Tell God you do.

Live as if it's so.

2. "*Do not grieve the Holy Spirit*" (Eph. 4:30).

Don't go against His perfect wishes, offending Him with grief.

Don't sin.

May I turn that around and make the second step to

daily and constant filling a one-word command:

CONFESS.

Because we do fail, we must know what it means to keep fellowship clean, by confessing all known sin.

Make it a habit to confess sin right away. As you do, God forgives.

The grief of the Spirit is removed.

And the sin.

Sadly, we have lost the art of confession when we glibly recite, "And if I have sinned in any way, please forgive me."

Real confession calls sin sin—with sorrow—and determines to stay away from it (2 Cor. 7:10).

3. "*Be filled with the Holy Spirit*" (Eph. 5:18).

The first time I typed that verse, it came out, "Be filled with the Holy Sport." That's easy—and prevalent!

It happens with money, cars, houses, clothes. We can be controlled by so many lords!

But the idea Paul wants to communicate here is this:

BE OPEN.

God calls us to be filled with His Holy Spirit or, in other words, to be open to His leadership and strength in every area of life.

You open yourself to the Holy Spirit when by faith you release control of your physical, spiritual, mental, and social life to Him. It's seeking to do what He wants you to do, as the Scriptures direct.

Many get scared by the word *filled.* It brings to their minds thoughts of six ounces or sixteen ounces, a little or a lot of the Spirit. They remember stories of people begging God to have more of His Spirit, or to get a feeling of His special joy.

Filling is not that.

It starts with knowing you are the Lord's and He is

yours, and that you have the Spirit of God living within you. Then it involves sacrificing your every ambition to His control.

Instead of His being one slice of the pie, He becomes the center and Lord of all.

And it shows.

You are open to Him.

And it is good!

4. "*Walk by the Spirit*" (Gal. 5:16).

Any other direction is dangerous.

WALK.

It's a clear command, repeated, and very practical. Very daily.

When you walk:

YOU OBEY YOUR HEAD! The body responds as the brain says move. There's something very wrong if the feet are not doing what the head says.

Spiritual walking is in obedience to the Head, Jesus Christ.

YOU GO ONE DIRECTION. Walking is not meant for circles.

Spiritual walking is related to commitment and direction too. Paul talks about "press[ing] toward the mark" (Phil. 3:14).

THE BODY WORKS TOGETHER. While legs get most of the credit, the whole body really works together in a walk. Lungs pump air, the heart supplies blood, the arms create balance. . . .

Spiritual walking is related to unity. One Christian loving Christ and walking in the Spirit is going to work together with the body. Unity is seen in the local church.

In church, in the body, Christians walk together, united and led by the same Head. The hand does not fight the foot!

THE BODY GOES ONE STEP AT A TIME. And we all walk in

the Spirit the same way—one step at a time.

A teenager praying for God's will about his vocation, but not obeying the Lord and walking in the Spirit, will not get to where God wants him to be unless he takes the next step: obeying now.

Walking in the Spirit means you are consciously seeking to obey the Lord, one step at a time, doing what is right. Now.

Then tomorrow. Then the next day.

Sometimes when you go for a walk, it is with special joy. A sunny beach . . . a quiet woods.

Other times you walk because it is necessary. You may not enjoy the walk, but you are getting from one place to another nonetheless.

In the same way, sometimes when you walk in the Spirit, doing what He directs you to do in His Word, it is with great joy. A special way to help someone you love . . . a chance to give time or money to a special interest . . . a warm worship experience.

But other times you take the step necessary because you are commanded. Feeling like it is not the point! You are walking in the Spirit to get from here to there.

To be the kind of person the Holy Spirit wants you to be.

Walk!

Walking in the Spirit involves choice.

We never get away from that, and shouldn't even want to!

Some of us would prefer to have a set of heavenly headphones or a Pollyanna health plan. We cling to the idea that God will whisper directions and give shortcuts.

That's not the way people walk in the Holy Spirit.

They choose.

Choice is a beautiful gift, expressing love and causing growth.

If you told a parent you had a magic pill to feed his child, so that the child would always automatically obey, the wise parent would (or should!) refuse it.

Love includes choice! No one gets warmed by the doll that says, "I love you" when you pull its string!

And God wants us to choose to love Him and walk under the orders of His Spirit, to exercise the gift of free will and obey biblical life-principles. Day after day.

We make the giant choice: to present our bodies and obey the Spirit in every area of life. Then every day we choose to walk in the Spirit by deciding to do what is right one step at a time.

Choice is a beautiful gift, and it cannot be returned.

It can be used in a very special way for the glory of the Lord.

For walking in the Spirit.

It is the first-string, joyful way to walk!

One step at a time.

6

RUNNING WITH ENDURANCE

"But we have this treasure in earthen vessels, that the surpassing greatness of the power may be of God and not from ourselves; we are afflicted in every way, but not crushed; perplexed, but not despairing; persecuted, but not forsaken; struck down, but not destroyed; always carrying about in the body the dying of Jesus, that the life of Jesus also may be manifested in our body."

(2 Cor. 4:7-10)

I began running—I'm talking physical again—as a little boy. It was even before it was a fad, before John Kennedy got people running in Washington, D.C. and around the country.

My father and I would drink a mixture of wheat germ and water, then run on a dirt road behind our house. I don't know why I did it, except that I admired my father and thought that he was mighty healthy for an old man, then in his late 20s.

Maybe that early experience made it easier to come back to running when I was in my 30s. A neighbor whom I'd met playing basketball at the Y suggested that we meet early in the morning to do some running. I decided the camaraderie would be good, and we made a pact. Secretly, I always hoped it would be raining, because we canceled then.

What I'm trying to say is that though running was in my blood early, it never has been all that much fun. Not in itself.

I accepted Jesus Christ as my Saviour when I was very young. I'd say age four or five if you put me on the spot. I can picture the evening, kneeling beside my bed with my grandmother and praying to trust Christ.

While I have doubted me a lot of times since then, I have not doubted Him.

That doesn't make it any easier to serve Him in my 40s, nor did it in my 30s or 20s.

My point is that it's always a choice and it's always a strain. True, you can read about people who act as if it's always fun to obey Jesus. I don't think they're lying. I just don't think they're telling the whole truth.

I mean I don't think they're dealing with some true feelings that are there. But let it be always fun for them.

For me it is often fun and always choice and usually work.

I think maybe we have made so much of how nice it is to trust Jesus that we need to concern ourselves a little more with how good it is and how right it is, however hard.

None of us would stoop to the level of the TV preacher who says that everybody ought to be happy and healthy—well, some of us would, at least the TV preacher!—but it's still easy to talk about how nice it is to follow Jesus and forget that we're also to take up a cross. That's really what it means to follow Jesus.

Somewhere, balance.

Of course, you get eternal life and joy and peace. And the abundant life is part of the package if you really obey.

But it's also buffeting your body and your evil nature and taking up your cross and allowing God to prune you when He may not prune somebody who doesn't want to grow for Him.

So it's not all that easy. It's not all that wonderful.

But it's all good.

To run with endurance is to run with a load on your back. To keep the weights on sometimes.

To run with endurance means to "remain under," to stay beneath the load. To keep going.

Think about it as remaining under a problem. Not down and out, but not running away from it either. Carrying the load for as long as you need to.

The promise from Scripture is that the load will never be too heavy. You can make it. You can do it!

But the promise is also that ultimately the load will be lifted.

Keep running. "Remain under."

Feel like it or not!

I don't always feel like a pastor. I doubt that our President looks in the White House mirror and exclaims each morning, "Now, that's a President!"

But he is one and he must do the work of one.

And he can.

I am a pastor and there are times when, feel like it or not, it is time to decide something.

Laughing inside, I remember a small task force meeting that had stalled, and I wondered why someone didn't get us to a decision. Then I remembered: *I* was the chairman. *I* was the one who needed to get the meeting moving.

Sometimes it is that way in life.

When you're running in a race and the first cramp hits or the mental fatigue or the shortness of breath, you have to make some tough decisions. Normally you can run through those things, perhaps slowing up a bit to a steadier pace, or perhaps simply getting your mind on something else.

One marathon runner told me that if he thinks about leg cramps, he's finished. Kaput.

But if he thinks about the goal and keeps his mind on enduring, he can usually run through the pain.

He remains under it until it goes away.

"Let us lay aside every weight, and the sin which does so easily beset us, and let us run with patience the race that is set before us" (Heb. 12:2, KJV).

Run with determination and long-suffering. Looooooong-suffering. The kind that keeps you faithfully attending church even when you don't feel like going.

The kind that helps you be open about the pain you are experiencing without giving up because life is hard.

Life is pain. Life is a swamp at times.

If you don't remain under, you'll circumvent the real purpose of your life. It may be that God allows that pain or will make a tremendous difference because of it.

Remaining under doesn't mean that you wish for pain or that you like it. It doesn't mean that you smile when you don't feel like it.

I never did understand why those song leaders try to make you smile on the second verse when the second verse is all about the fiery trials.

But you can keep going and remain faithful. And remain under by carrying the load.

Jesus did. According to Hebrews 12:2, "For the joy set before Him [He] endured the cross, despising the shame, and has sat down at the right hand of the throne of God"—a phrase meaning that He has all authority, that He finished His task.

He remained under.

He kept at it.

So can I.

Runners today have better food, better training, better coaches, better equipment.

Not to mention the human factor. We are producing better individuals. Stronger wills.

Maybe it's because the gold is so rewarding, and to get on the back of the Wheaties box can secure a lifetime income. Or maybe it's because we have learned in many ways, especially in sports, to control the human will.

I'm not down on sports—you already knew that. But the Christian ought to lead the pack when it comes to self-discipline and motivation. Probably we have yet to see—and this is an old quote—what God will do with a man who is totally dedicated to Him.

There's something about physical running that is the same for everyone. Everyone needs oxygen. Everyone needs training. Everyone's got to have some muscle in the legs and a few other places.

But then there is something that can't be measured. It doesn't come inhaling oxygen or by eating the right food the day before. This is motivation.

This is the choice. The act of faith.

This determination comes from the mind or the heart. The will. Runners tested on certain endurance machines can last anywhere from 1 to 100 minutes before petering out. Army psychologists report that some individuals who undergo grueling aerobic programs throw in the towel after only a matter of minutes, while others are still hanging in an hour later.

What's the difference? The difference is the size of their "wanna," their will.

The same is true in the Christian life. One man faces a criticism from another and blows up. A fist fight results, or at least a verbal split.

Another man handles a similar criticism without hostility or bitterness. He seems to have the mind of Christ.

It's not all in the makeup of their genes. Some of it is simply will and decision to trust God's way as best.

And that's the way to live all of life. The way to run. The way to obey.

It was a shorter race, but I was in less-than-the-best shape early that spring. (My jogging in the winter isn't quite as aggressive as when the weather warms up.) I turned to the runner beside me. "Tell me I can make it," I said. My familiar plea.

He didn't know me, but he was willing to lend a voice. "You can make it."

I didn't know whether to believe him or not. But endurance simply means taking another step followed by another, and piling them all on top of each other.

Even going up a hill, I leaned over and took shorter steps, and kept letting those words echo around my brain and my heart. Especially my heart.

Endurance comes from the heart. It is the muscles of the will saying that because Christ is Lord and gives us hope and rewards faithfulness, we will refuse to drop out. We must keep going.

Nobody has it especially easy.

People who always try to make the Christian life hunky-dory are living in some kind of a superficial shell that keeps them from touching the lives of persons with cancer, persons without jobs, or men and women feeling the pain of marital problems.

Or the families starving in the deserts of Africa.

But nevertheless we are able to live with victory, and the triumph of Christ. And that's special.

You run with endurance because you *will* to run with endurance. You keep at it because you *decide* to keep at it.

Yes, there is strength in God's Spirit. Yes, there is power through His Word. Yes, there is the supernatural.

But there is also the will. And the will keeps the machine moving.

The hill looked like a mile and a half. I think it's actually about a third that long. It was part of the course of the "Potato Stomp" at Mantua, Ohio—9.3 miles from start to finish.

And this hill, which comes somewhere around mile seven, seems like an eternity. To be honest, I think my time was something like eternity. All the way up you think, "I can't do this."

My mind goes back to the children's story about the choo-choo train that thought he could and thought he could and thought he could.

I think he was loco!

But I made it to the top because I remained under.

A band was assembled at the peak. I thought I was in heaven! I smiled and started down the other side of the hill with delight.

Problems don't always have bands playing the Notre Dame fight song as you struggle through them, but they often get resolved with special peace.

And you are so glad you endured.

When I was a boy, it was that way when I went to the dentist. My mother always told me to think about how good it would feel when it was over.

Sometimes the hard problems of life are like those childhood visits to the dentist. I need to make a difficult phone call and I really don't want to because the first sentences will be hard, but I'm so glad when I've done it.

And maybe someone's been helped!

I need to confront my child with some parental wisdom vital to her maturity.

Confrontation is not my favorite pastime.

But remaining under means doing it in spite of the pain. It means doing what is best even if it hurts.

And because I commit to remain under, God sees to it that I come out on top spiritually.

Keep going. Keep doing what is right. Endure.

It is my opinion—so get ready to argue if you like—that we make too much ado about the kind of sentiment implied in the expression, "Let go and let God."

Let God do what?

Let go of your worries and let God have them? Great. Let go of your sins and let God forgive them? Excellent. That's His whole idea.

Let go of your grudges and let God be the Judge? Right on. He is in charge of that whole section too.

Let go of your responsibilities and let God take care of them? Let go of the need for discipline and hope God gives you strength in spite of your apathy? Let go of your drive to be stronger in Christ and let God give you the growth instead?

No, no, no!

"I didn't do anything—it was all God," a speaker said to me after I thanked him for how much his talk had helped me.

I wanted to get in on that plan so I wouldn't have so much prep time.

You know what I'm saying. In my opinion, running the Christian race includes a whole lot of discipline and stretching, not yawning and acting as if it all depends on God.

Certainly He is the giver of every good and perfect gift. Certainly He deserves the glory for all that is accomplished.

But just as certainly, He gives His strength in special

ways to those who realize their weaknesses, but discipline themselves to control their weaknesses and do His will.

They stretch. They design their lives so that they can draw on His power, but also so that they can take care of their impotence. They don't just lie around and let their weird or lazy lusts run away with them.

They buffet their bodies.

Paul essentially says, "I give my body a black eye. I bring it into subjection. I want it to obey."

Certainly he is talking about his sin nature. Self-control means grabbing ourselves by the neck and saying, "This is the way we are going to go."

Every physical runner who trains in the morning knows exactly what I mean. When the alarm rings, he or she turns and mumbles, "Who, me?"

Those snooze alarms are wonderful inventions. Press them and they give you nine more minutes.

You can do that for three days if you like. . . .

But a person who is going to enjoy life and get the best out of it is going to take that body and get it up and get it dressed and get it on the road or on the job or into the Word or whatever is first on the agenda.

"Bod, you're coming with me," self-will says. "I'm in charge. I'm not going to let my feelings run away with me.

"Or rather, lie away with me."

Running the Christian race involves discipline. It involves hard work.

The self-discipline that means subjection to Jesus Christ also includes subjection of our wills. And that, for me, is work.

Maybe I'm more selfish than you are. Maybe I inherited something you didn't.

But I suspect we are all in the same boat when it comes to needing the disciplines of the Christian life, understanding exactly what Paul means when he says that sometimes he wants to do right, but he doesn't want to; and sometimes he doesn't want to do wrong, but he does want to. We all identify with the skirmishes of Romans 7 and the pain of buffeting in 1 Corinthians 9 and the inner battle of Galatians 5.

"The flesh sets its desire against the Spirit" (Gal. 5:17).

Very few people who read that verse have any trouble making a personal application.

They just finished looking at a picture of a beautiful woman in a magazine and deciding if they were going to stare the wrong way.

They just finished hearing someone say a bitter word toward them and deciding if they were going to make the situation twice as bad by retaliating.

They just finished learning how they could cheat a little bit on their finances and no one would ever know, not even the IRS.

The flesh wars against the Spirit, and there is skirmish, and there is struggle.

To run in obedience to Christ, one must say, "I will. I really want to obey."

Sometimes in the middle of a race, I hear my body whispering to my will, "What is the sense of this, buddy?

"Why in the world would you want to drive me like this?

"Wouldn't you like to just lie down over there in the shade and forget this whole thing? Think of the joy it would be to stretch out with a lemonade or to walk up in the stands and buy that cotton candy and watch the rest of the runners?"

"Not so," I must respond. "It would feel better now, but not in the long run."

It may be profitable for a short time, but we're looking for the long gain.

For the long haul!

"A long obedience in the same direction," to use Eugene Peterson's pertinent phrase!

Run with discipline. Decide it's best. It is for many reasons, especially the eternal ones.

But even right now.

So many who have given in to the wretched lusts of the flesh have ruined so much. A Christian leader or pastor bombs morally and he throws away seventeen years of ministry and 700 people who were looking to him as a spiritual profile.

Two married people have had enough of each other, file the divorce papers, and for the next twenty-five years wish they had taken the time to get counsel and work out their differences.

Yes the pain is hard, but yes there is pure delight, giant joy when you cross the finish line and know you've completed the race.

I scream back at my body then, "See! I knew it would be better to finish. Am I ever glad I did not give in."

The biblical use of analogies can get us on hobby horses if we take them to extremes. For example, Paul sometimes speaks of the Christian life as a crucifixion and sometimes as a wrestling match. Let's not stretch either analogy beyond its limits. There is no way you can parallel the spiritual journey exactly. But there is resting in Christ. There is letting Christ live in you. There is discipline. There is struggle.

It all works together as we honor Jesus Christ as Lord.

So why don't our bodies want to cooperate?

They are weak. They want to take the easiest route.

Watch yourself when you are on a diet or trying to discipline yourself in the simple matter of not drinking much caffeine. It's a classic illustration of the battle that takes place.

A friend who had come to Christ in my presence was grappling with a very difficult problem of morality, a habit that he had not kicked from before conversion. He put me on the spot when he asked what one thing I was fighting in the area of self-control so that I could go through this struggle with him.

Maybe it was a time when I wasn't facing giant crises, or maybe I wasn't being transparent enough, but I agreed that I would give up Pepsi during the time he was giving up his worst habit.

I was drinking too much of the stuff, and I knew I should give it up anyway.

So for thirty days I was not allowed to touch it. Not one drop.

I did fine for a week. Two weeks.

Almost three.

And then my thoughtless family, not seeming to care, put some Pepsi in the refrigerator for themselves. Doesn't anybody love anybody around here?

A few evenings later, when my wife was upstairs and the kids were in their rooms, I started to fall. My will started to quiver. You wouldn't have noticed if you were filming it, but inside I was gradually becoming a dishrag. There was Pepsi in that refrigerator, and I had not tasted any for approximately eighteen days.

What would it matter if I took a little bit?

Would the world stop turning?

Would it ruin God's sovereign plan?

All was quiet. I carefully opened the refrigerator. I looked around—no cameras like those used by banks or quick-shop stores on the lookout for thieves. No family.

I could not even sense God's presence.

I took the bottle to my lips. Almost there. My arm knew exactly what to do. My stomach was preparing. My tastebuds were clapping.

Just then, around the corner, as if sent by the enemy, came my wife.

I was caught.

Caught with a bottle almost to my lips and a will almost

shriveled and. . . .

How weak I am.

If I can't lick something like that, how can I lick my selfish nature? How can I keep from drinking in the lusts of the world and the pride of life and the selfishness that is all around?

Only through a walk with Christ. Only by remaining under by His grace.

Only as I walk in the Spirit and stay in the Scriptures and believe that His way is much better than mine.

I do believe that. I do want that.

One of the great lessons of life is to admit weakness. To admit that though we really do not want to sin, we really do want to sin.

Maybe then we can arrive with the Apostle Paul at another great biblical truth sequential to this—that in our weakness we are made strong. When we admit we are proud, we at least are on the first step toward abiding in Christ in that area.

When we admit that we can't conquer something, we at least are raising our hand and calling for grace.

And so Paul tells us to remain under and keep going and to look to Christ for help.

Pick up those feet and get going. One step at a time.

With endurance.

Marathon runners say that the first twenty miles of the twenty-six are half the race. Some even add, "Anyone can run twenty miles. But it's like starting all over to run the last six—and then there's the last 385 yards."

Anyone can take certain pains in life, or certain temptations. But the issue is when the hard ones hit.

When you're really hurt by someone's criticisms, and have an easy way to get back at him.

When the temptation is very clear, and you're out of town.

When the cheating is easy, and no one will ever miss the money.

That's when endurance comes in. That's when you need God's Spirit. That's when you need the drive to do what's right.

That's when you're ready to stretch, and God's Spirit is ready to help, and you can do it by His grace.

Some people with physical burdens such as cancer or blindness or quadriplegia face the negative with resolve and become strong through it and grow in grace. They focus on Christ.

Others get bitter. They double their problems.

Those who choose to run with endurance come out strong, and they seem to know Christ better.

When Paul persistently prayed to Christ to deliver him from his thorn in the flesh, the answer was repeatedly no. That's not the kind of answer anybody wants.

But he remained under. He accepted God's will for his life.

And he found that in that physical weakness, whatever it was, he got strong.

He got strong because he admitted that he was weak. That made him dependent.

Pride goes before a fall because pride makes you act like you don't need help. And since you do, you don't make it.

I love the promise in Isaiah 40:31: "Yet those who wait for the Lord will gain new strength; they will mount up with wings like eagles, they will run and not get tired, they will walk and not become weary."

Those who wait on Him are the ones who serve Him by asking, "What would You like this evening?"

The word *wait* can also refer to spiritual resolve to sit at His feet, seek His strength, and do His bidding.

The promise is threefold: He will help us fly like an eagle at times.

Or run, but not get tired.

Or barely walk—but not faint.

And Christ has stood with us all as we have looked to Him and tried not to faint, and He has made it so.

Yes, He runs with us.

Sometimes, indeed, we soar like the eagle, and we feel that life is so special. We're ready to sing songs, all four verses.

Other times, and I'm using Haddon Robinson's beautiful analogy from this verse, He has given me grace to run with Him and not get so tired that I couldn't keep going. Those are days when my effort seemed to blend with His grace and things got accomplished. I ran. We ran. We did it together. By the exertion of discipline and the hard work of late hours or stretching to have nerve to call someone to Christ or to heal a problem, I've run. Christ has run with me. I don't get tired. We make it to the end of the project or the building program or the day, and it seems that His strength has been so lasting.

That is God's grace and provision.

But other times I have been able to take just another step. I felt that way in a three-month period of depression over a major decision, a situation I talked about earlier in this book. My first time in that kind of enduring valley. I could not understand it.

Yet I did not faint.

And that too was from God's hand. He is special.

He runs with me.

When you reach the end of your spiritual steam, it feels like you just breathed your last breath.

Something inside yells to quit.

It's not God and it's not the devil. It's part of you.

We're made that way. Quitters.

Such is death.

But we can keep going. Often I have heard an inner

voice insist that this could be my last gasp, that I couldn't possibly go further. And yet I have gone further.

I tricked him. I tricked me? I took charge. I told me what to do!

Mind over matter?

Spirit over body or nature?

Something like that. I refuse to spend too many hours trying to figure it out. I just know I can will to keep going in those situations.

And the size of my "wanna" determines how many steps I keep going.

7

YOUR RACE IS NOT MY RACE

"Therefore, since we have so great a cloud of witnesses surrounding us, let us also lay aside every encumbrance, and the sin which so easily entangles us, and let us run with endurance the race that is set before us."

(Heb. 12:1)

"So then each one of us shall give account of himself to God. The faith which you have, have as your own conviction before God. Happy is he who does not condemn himself in what he approves."

(Rom. 14:12, 22)

There were still lepers who were not cleansed, cripples who could not walk, blind people who could not see. There were still many who had not believed.

And yet Jesus could say at the end of His life on earth, or close to it, "I have finished the work which Thou gave Me to do" (John 17:4, KJV).

And on the cross: "It is finished!" (John 19:30)

How could He make such declarations when there was still work to be done?

But notice that Jesus did not say *all* the work was done (though certainly all the work necessary for salvation was done).

He simply said that as a person He had done the work that God the Father had given Him to do with His earthly life.

That's all I can do. I can't win the world. I have to drop my messianic complex just as you do. I can't finish everything in a day. I don't think there has ever been a day in my life when I went away from the office or finished something in the evening and felt like I was done. Caught up.

Not many people have that luxury. Certainly not a homemaker. Certainly not a doctor.

Certainly not anyone who cares about witnessing.

And yet Jesus could unashamedly say, "I have finished the work You gave Me to do." He was running *His* race. He wasn't running everywhere in the world. He was doing what God wanted *Him* to do. He was being faithful where He was. In His world.

Your world, my world. The people you know and the places you go.

I can be faithful in my world, and therefore I can run the race God has set before me. By His sovereignty, He makes that race clear as the day unfolds, and I get to respond as well as act.

Paul's words to Timothy echo Jesus': "I have fought the

good fight, I have finished the course" (2 Tim. 4:7).

There were still places Paul might have wished to go and evangelize and more letters he could have written!

But he knew that such was not in God's plan. Paul had finished the course God had laid out *for him.*

That was enough. That's all God asks. I don't have to be Billy Graham. I don't have to win the city overnight. I don't have to stack myself up against somebody whom I know is better than me—or worse.

I just need to be me, in the presence and power of Christ.

Charlie Brown is one of my favorite theologians! In one of the "Peanuts" cartoon TV specials, Charlie Brown is preparing for the great mile run. He is determined to win. Four times around the track, and he's got it.

So Charlie practices and practices the first twenty-six minutes of the program. Then comes the big race.

Uh oh. Charlie's in the lead at the beginning. But the gate at the end of the oval is open, and Charlie, without thinking, runs straight instead of turning. He's out into the countryside. He turns to see if anyone is behind him. "No one," he says. "I'm winning!"

Come back, Charlie Brown. You're going the wrong way!

You've picked your own course. You're off the oval.

Come back to the cinders!

And such is life for so many. We get a break or do something well and then get cocky about it and go the wrong direction. The way of Christ is back there at the track. It may not be as exciting running in circles at times. But it may be God's way for us.

Thank you, Charlie Brown. You remind me to stay on course.

To run the race God puts before me.

The day I stop comparing myself with others is the day I

stop feeling lustful when another church is more successful, or proud when ours beats another.

The goal of life is simply to be faithful to Christ, and to do what He wants me to do. For you to do what He wants you to do.

Your race is not my race.

My race is not your race.

In its most direct application or interpretation, the phrase, "Let us run . . . the race that is set before us," in Hebrews 12:1 indicates a single pathway. The straight and narrow. The way of Jesus Christ for *us*.

In one sense we all run the same race.

Run the way of Christ.

There are, of course, many options. The believer is faced every day with a new decision of whether or not to obey the command of Romans 12:1. The word *present* may imply conclusiveness—a once-for-all action—but everybody knows of the turnoffs. Indeed, we have all taken them now and then.

To run the race set before you is to stay on course. To decide that His way is really best. There are times when I let my mind slip into something very selfish or lustful, even though I know it won't get me anywhere spiritually. The best cure for me as God's Spirit convicts is to think bottom line. Just what would come of that thought if I followed through? Where would it get me? What would it do to my church and my family? And how would it affect my Saviour's name and mine? I guess that's called considering the consequences.

Choosing to run the race set before you, the race of Christ, the correct way of living according to Scripture, is reinforced when you think where it gets you in the end.

The writer of Hebrews talks about that when he says that we are to follow the pattern of our spiritual leaders "considering the outcome of their way of life" (Heb. 13:7, NIV).

Look what they end up like!

Hebrews 11 is all about such people too. They went through a lot of hardships, but they surely came out on top. In heaven too!

It's fun to meet new people at 10K races. I find most of them very healthy. I think that's what started me jogging in the first place. That and the fact that I was losing my breath in the third sermon Sunday mornings.

As I realized that men and women who kept down their weight seemed to be happier and healthier, and as I read books that said these folks would stay around longer, I considered their outcome and I began to run.

People who run the straight and narrow with Christ are going to be people who are closer to Him.

And that's the place to be!

But another way to look at Hebrews 12:1, taking a little liberty, is to think about "the race set before [*me*]" as opposed to the race set before Charlie Sedgewicks.

I'm not supposed to run Charlie's race. I'm responsible to do what I'm responsible to do.

I don't have to be Charlie. I don't have to be better than Charlie.

I just need to run the race God sets before me.

I don't have to judge anybody else's race. I only need to critique my own. And when I finish my race, God will judge me and probably won't even ask my help in evaluating my fellow believers.

I'm to run the race set before *me*.

For example, when I am criticized, I might not necessarily need to change. If it's valid criticism, fine; I should take steps to improve my behavior. But if I know I'm following God's will, and somebody is merely harping about my independent stance or convictions or about the way I did something, I can keep running. It's not his race I have to run. It's not his finish tape I have to break. It's not his crown I'm going to enjoy.

It's the race set before me by Christ.

When I switched pastorates, the decision process was fourteen months of sheer agony, because I was so deeply in love with my previous pastorate of fifteen years. Looking back, friend-wife and I see God's hand overriding every step along the way, but in the middle of the decision I certainly did not feel peace.

I was ready to quit everything.

Even running.

In fact, for a while I didn't have much strength to run. I lost seventeen pounds and would often hear my daughters say at the meal table, "Please eat something."

Some who criticized that I was even thinking about the change said that I couldn't possibly follow through with the move. They reminded me of the healthy circumstances of the other church (the kind that make you ask, "Where does a church like that go from here?").

It became a lonely decision. But then, many are like that. I'm not striking my case as unusual! I'm just saying that in the middle of the criticism and the questioning in my own mind, I had to recognize that this was a time for Jeanine and me to decide the race that was set before me. No cheerleaders were allowed to vote. Certainly, I could take advice from my friends.

But *I* had to make the decision.

I know such lonely decisions are prevalent, and hope that this incident from my own life might get you thinking about your personal race. There are times when others do not understand. There are times when criticism makes you want to quit running or to follow the crowd.

The easiest thing to do is often wrong.

Pity a person who bounces with every Gallup Poll and changes his convictions to what the neighbors or office workers think. Even when the whole world goes another way, you must run the race as you see God directing.

Such people become leaders, but they also become strong followers and servants in a local church. They give of themselves.

Don't run your friend's race. Don't do what your grandmother told you to do just because she told you. See if it's the race that God has set before you in Scripture. See if it's God's best for your life and the use of your gifts for His glory. Then run!

In the film, *Chariots of Fire*, Eric Liddell's father wisely advises his son, "Eric, run fast and let the whole world sit back and wonder." Eric did that. He stayed with his convictions, and he stood alone in that Olympic decision not to run on Sunday. He ran the spiritual race set before him as his conscience had been set. And he ran beautifully, for God's glory.

Be sure you are committed to such a high calling. God's race for you is the best race in the whole wide world. It is like no other. You'll never be happier than in His will.

Before Jesus ascended into heaven after the Resurrection, He and Peter had a heart-to-heart talk on the beach. At one point in the conversation, Jesus told Peter how he would die: "You will stretch out your hands, and someone else will gird you, and bring you where you do not wish to go" (John 21:18).

Then He simply told Peter, "Follow Me!" (v. 19)

Peter, inquisitive candid Peter, saw John standing there and wondered, "What about this man?" (v. 21)

Jesus answered, "If I want him to remain until I come, what is that to you? You follow Me!" (v. 22)

In essence, Christ said, "John's My business. You take care of your own life!"

In football, someone wins and someone loses. In competitive running, it is also a contest, but with an added element. You are in a contest with yourself, not just with the other people. You are testifying (from the Latin word for *contest*) to who you are.

You don't lose if you do your best.

The same is true in our lives in Christ.

We are not racing against each other. I don't have to be as good a preacher as my predecessor. You are not in a contest with the alto who stands next to you in the choir.

We are simply to testify what kind of people we are. That is the contest. We are to witness to the fact that we can be what God means us to be.

And the witnesses who are there in the stands are people who testified to what God did in their lives. Moses is not better than David. David is not better than Jacob. Jacob is not better than Sarah. They were all in the contest. And so are we.

The contest is to show who we are in Christ. It is to bring out the best in us.

Maybe the saddest news of all, and I'm not announcing anything new here, is that many people will miss what they are made to be in life.

They will miss the point. They'll simply not have linked with God as their Creator and Lord.

Some people pay to go through college and come out with a B.A., but hardly anything else. It's easy to go through a day and never have a moment of joy or of contribution to others.

The nice thing is that it's never too late. The prodigal can come home whenever he wishes. The sinner can find new birth at the moment of trust. All of us can be renewed as we come back to obedience. It is God's way. His middle name is forgiveness.

His first name is power. The Almighty God is willing and able to show His mercy. His kindnesses are there all the time.

And the Good News is that He wants to spread this message around the world through you and me. The Gospel is wrapped up in the power and forgiveness of a Holy God who by His wisdom sent His Son to give His life so that forgiveness could be granted on a daily basis.

And one day future, the power will shift into high gear, and Christ will return, and all those forgiven ones will live and reign in power with Him.

That will be some race!

The church of Christ today is plagued with comparisons. Christians try to "dress up" every other Christian the way they "dress." I call such gatherings "uniform" meetings.

Sure, there are some things that are clear for all Christians, but on other things we can be flexible.

For instance, lying and gossip are out for everyone. Murder and adultery have no place. All of us are called to know Christ, to get into His Word, and to spread the Gospel.

In that sense, the race set before us means trust and obedience in Christ, and it's the same for all of us. We are to love each other because we love Him. And when His love fills us, it shows in our unity on the major issues.

But on the minor issues, there is room for difference. Each person has his or her own life, in Christ, to live—his or her own duties, obligations, and goals.

Run that race and don't look over your shoulder at others.

Run that race and be faithful *yourself!*

When the Scripture says, "Whatever your hand finds to do . . . do it with all your might" (Ecc. 9:10), it is telling us to really live.

It doesn't mean that you have to run at full steam all the time. A runner is crazy if he goes out and runs at dash speed for a marathon.

He will die after a hundred yards or maybe a mile if he's in shape.

What Solomon means here is to run with intensity. To

know you are doing the right thing. To run with wisdom.

Life is to be lived that way.

A man is crazy if he goes full tilt seven days a week. The pace will eventually kill him. But to choose the best things in order to do them the best ways—that is sensible living.

In short, life is simply choosing to do one thing instead of another. There's always a smorgasbord of options. So you get to choose.

And let's hear none of this nonsense about God telling you what to do. Sure, there are times when He has done that. But today we have His Scriptures which tell us what to do. We must choose on the basis of what He has revealed in His Word, taking to heart the divine wisdom that's contained therein.

The physical runner is in a similar situation. No one makes him go the next step. He knows the race and the course, but he has to make the effort. He gets encouragement from people around him and water is available at each mile marker in some races, but he must run and choose.

Such is life.

But it's good. The more you choose to do what's right, the more you can go. A second wind comes, a stirring within that says that because of the successes you've already achieved, you can go to the end.

I love that feeling.

I don't run enough to get that real runner's high very often, but I know the joy of getting my three miles in and feeling good that I did at least that. I also know the joy of doing what I should do for someone else, or apologizing when I should, or saying, "I love you," or getting the work done in the best way I can.

And then finishing my day with a clean conscience, and the marriage bed undefiled. Even my stomach feels good.

Such is life when I live it in Christ. And that's the way it's meant to be.

Choosing the best thing because there are always many things. Choosing the right thing because there are always many wrong things. But not getting "hyper" about it. Simply doing what's right and doing it best, with all your might.

That is life. That is the way to run.

And then at the end of life, you will be able to hold your head high and say some of the most satisfying words anybody could possibly say: "I have finished the work You gave me to do."

"I have finished the course."

"I have run the race set before me."

8

RUN AFTER LOVE

"Love is patient, love is kind, and is not jealous; love does not brag and is not arrogant, does not act unbecomingly; it does not seek its own, is not provoked, does not take into account a wrong suffered, does not rejoice in unrighteousness, but rejoices with the truth; bears all things, believes all things, hopes all things, endures all things. Love never fails."

(1 Cor. 13:4-7, 8a)

"But now abide faith, hope, love, these three; but the greatest of these is love. Pursue love."

(1 Cor. 13:13–14:1a)

Experts are awed at some of the things that athletes are doing these days.

It can't just be the steroids!

The leaps and spins of a skater. The somersaults and agility of a gymnast. The speed and strength of the muscular lineman, who towers above people who played the same position in years gone by.

People can get pretty good at a lot of different things!

Onlookers sigh.

And pay big bucks to see them play.

Or buy the cereal they eat.

It's a whole other world, and maybe it has its place.

Some of it.

But what we need for sure are men and women who would get good at God's race:

Running after love.

It's interesting that Paul sums up his lesson on love in 1 Corinthians 13 with a couple of words that tell us simply to go after it.

(By the way, Paul did not divide 1 Corinthians 13 and 14 where they're divided. A guy in a horse-drawn carriage did that. According to the famous joke and legend, every time the carriage bounced, he made a verse, and every time the horse jerked, he divided a chapter!)

After the apostle's grand finale when all the fireworks are going out, after he runs out of words to describe love, after he has even drawn two other giant words into the chapter—*faith* and *hope* (and we know we're lost without those two), Paul says, "But the greatest of these is love.

"Pursue love."

Go after it. Make it your ambition. Make it your goal.

Run for all you're worth after love. As you go, think of the finish line and of the great stretch in your spirit called love.

God created us to do many of the things that He does,

especially in the areas of love and forgiveness. That isn't as true of some of His other attributes. For example, we can be creative and that's a bit like God, but *He* made human beings and a universe. We're into writing books or designing dresses or building buildings. The scale is vastly different.

But in the area of forgiveness, we can totally forgive someone. We can love him. We can do what God would be doing if He were near that person.

That's the beauty of being human and yet, at once, being God's child. That's the pleasure of having His Spirit within our spirit.

When a man shows love, he is really doing what God values. He is coming to his highest place on this earth.

We can praise God and worship Him, and that's really at the top of our job description.

But love is right up there too. We praise Him when we love. We show His excellence. We show His worth. We get His help.

Pursue love!

Everything else is an empty chase.

Like the man who climbed the ladder of success and got to the top and found out it was leaning against the wrong building, runners who go after all the other things in life are going to miss it.

"Go for the gusto," the world shouts. "You only go around once in life." "Be all that you can be."

But love is bigger than all of that. It's more than just selfish ambition—in fact, it's getting outside our own selfish ambitions to be what God means us to be.

That is the joy of life. That is the purpose.

Pursue love!

Get on your mark, get set . . .

Go after love!

There are a number of things we are to run after in life. The Bible is clear.

"*Pursue* these things" . . . and then it names righteousness, godliness, love, peace with all men.

The word *pursue* used here is taken from the word *persecute*. It means to go after and grab. "Don't just stand there! Go get it."

Why does God tell us to pursue such important character traits or actions? Couldn't we just sit in a nice chair or in a padded pew and watch it happen?

It won't happen.

Golf great Jack Nicklaus overheard an admirer remark, "I wish I could putt like that."

Nicklaus responded, "I didn't get that way by wishing."

Neither did the good pianist. Nor the excellent church usher. Nor the successful accountant.

People worked to get where they are. They willed to do right and learned how. Then they practiced and grew. They stretched. They groaned a little.

They failed and tried again.

Love is that way too. It will not come to us. We must pursue it.

I'm not sure if waiting for a feeling is ever a good response for a Christian, though I've seen people do it all the time. A husband and wife are at war in their marriage. Will they forgive each other? "I'm asking God to give me a sense of love; then I'll forgive her," the husband tells me. That "wait-and-see" attitude usually has tragic results.

So, why pursue love?

1. *We must pursue love because it is our opposite.* It's not a part of our human nature. God is love. And so He has an easy time loving. We are not love. And so we have a hard time giving and committing, reaching and stretching.

Good health or at least excellent conditioning is the opposite of what happens when we do what's normal.

Personally, I like apple pie. I could make it a steady diet. Eating sweets comes naturally to me. I'm attracted to them.

Of course, if I eat only what I feel like eating, I will not have any sense of conditioning or surge of discipline. I will get lazy and overweight. Naturally.

Same with love. If we just sit around and wonder if we should love or let our lazy bones determine our schedules, we won't pursue love. We won't pursue anything except selfish interests.

We must run after love in this discipline of life because it's our opposite and it needs to be pursued.

2. *We must run after love because it is excellent, the best way to live.*

When our hearts are right and we're thinking in tune with God, we really do want what's best. By God's Spirit, we have committed ourselves to a way of life that lasts forever.

"I show you a still more excellent way," writes Paul (1 Cor. 12:31). More excellent than preaching and prophecy and a lot of other things that are high on our pedestals.

It's the way of love. God wants us to run after it because it's so important in His eyes. So excellent in its virtue. It lasts forever! You can't say that about very many things.

People who really enjoy life and who are getting the best out of it are people who are pursuing love.

George Sweeting wrote in his book *Catch the Spirit of Love* that he wants his tombstone epitaph to read: "He pursued love."

Mark mine with the same chisel. It's the excellent way. Paul said it. Jesus said it. They both lived it. We can try too.

3. *We need to pursue love because it is a whole way of life.* "I show you a still more excellent *way*," says Paul. Not an act or a thing or a day, but a way.

A whole way of living. A way of love.

Most of us are characterized by some adjective or virtue.

Say Charlie's name and immediately someone thinks of anger or selfishness or pushiness or love or joy or frivolity.

What character trait describes you? Which best describes me?

We need to pursue love because it's not just a kind deed we do once in a while. It is not something we leave at the church door when we head for the car after the Sunday worship service.

It is a way of life. A good way.

The best way.

Dr. George Sheehan, one of the prophets of the benefits of running, has written a book entitled, *Running and Being.* In it he urges Americans to "spill out of the TV room after an event, and act on what they have seen." Sheehan himself has been known to "spill back onto the road for a second run of the day after being stimulated by a televised sporting event!"

Loving God and others ought to become so much the heartbeat of the believer that we seek opportunities to love or at least enjoy the ones God gives.

It's good for us. One of our reasons for being!

4. *We need to pursue love because it is urgent.*

We need it now!

The needs of the world around us are hard to ignore—at least for those of us intent on following the heart of God.

There is no time to lose. We have lost too much already.

If to *pursue* is to go and get and squeeze, this clearly implies a very willful and deliberate act.

All of this argues against the very prevalent "couldn't-help-it" attitude that people love to hang on to for dear life.

Their own dear lives.

Living for Christ is not all that easy. It's not always fun.

Of course, the idea of heaven always brings nice feelings, but the idea of stretching ourselves for pursuing love sounds too much like work.

Everyone who wins a gold medal at the Olympics stands up and receives it with great joy.

But that athlete gave up a lot and stretched a lot and

pursued excellence for many months before getting to that pinnacle of joy.

And sometimes all the hard work was for a few seconds of gold or silver or bronze recognition.

The best things in life are not always free. Some of the best things cost, but not usually money.

A good love relationship in a marriage is costly. Don't let anyone kid you. It doesn't mean buying your spouse jewelry and nice clothes, but it may cost time.

It may cost the will to win an argument.

It may cost the effort of unselfishness.

I don't know anyone for whom that comes easily.

Yet to pursue love is to direct yourself along that Christ-like way. To say that you really believe it's important. To put other things aside.

Jesus did, and He becomes our model.

He taught James and John not to seek to sit on His right hand or left, but to give their lives as servants. His exhortation to us is the same.

"The Son of man did not come to be served, but to serve, and to give His life a ransom for many" (Mark 10:45).

That's a costly choice.

That's action and not just talk.

Someone who really pursues love is going to give his time to others.

He isn't always going to talk about inconvenience.

He isn't always going to say that it's not the right time to do something for someone.

To pursue love is to make love your goal, and then to allow other things to fall in place.

Like the runner who has just finished his training run or the special race, one feels tired but good after doing something that took effort to help others.

I know a couple who are always looking to share their faith with others. She tries to start a group Bible study in the morning because he leads one in the afternoon or evening.

They pursue love, though they don't talk about it that way.

They just seek to share their faith.

They have a lot of the nice conveniences of life, and they take vacations pretty regularly, and sometimes they're chided about "suffering for Jesus."

But I think Jesus sees their stretching in love, and their pursuit of the godly goal of sharing their faith.

Maybe He throws in the other things to thank them.

No promise here. Sometimes when you pursue love you get only rejection.

But at least you're going after love and doing what Christ wants.

And, after all, everybody runs after something. Everybody agonizes to get somewhere in life.

Just before being martyred, Paul writes to Timothy, "I have fought the good fight" (2 Tim. 4:7). In essence, he says, "I have agonized the good agony."

The very best one, in fact.

The best agony is the agony to be like Christ, and that includes attractive holy love.

Pursue it. Go after it. Go get it. It won't come to you!

When we pursue holiness and the way of love that God wants us to have, we are willing to pump spiritual iron, to get into the Word and pray and take those endurance steps that get us another step closer.

It will take a lifetime. But it will be a good lifetime. It will be the good agony. The good fight.

Pursuing involves pressure and work and strain.

Pursuing love means that it is probably just a little bit out of our reach. It means that we're really leaning forward to get it.

We aren't born with the desire to love. We aren't filled with a spirit of compassion as we start out this life.

We have to run after it.

Many people pursue nothing but satisfaction.

It seems to me that if you run after satisfaction, you'll never quite get there. You'll live your life in the first eleven chapters of Ecclesiastes, where over and over again comes the phrase, "Vanity of vanities, all is vanity."

It just isn't there.

Look at Ecclesiastes 2 and see Solomon building all kinds of beautiful additions to his home and gathering to himself all kinds of wisdom and 700 wives and 300 concubines (can you imagine the tensions at home!) . . . and still concluding it was all a bunch of soap bubbles.

"Soap bubbles" is the way my Hebrew professor in seminary translated that word *vanity*.

I remember so clearly the first time our first daughter got to enjoy a bubble bath in the tub by herself. The mixture of the water with this miraculous potion had brought huge suds, and she thought it wonderful.

But a few minutes later we heard her crying.

We ran in. She explained.

"The bubbles are all gone! All gone."

Such is life in the empty vein.

On the other hand, the pursuit of love will usually be quite satisfying. Certainly, it hurts when people reject our love, but because this is the area where God wants us to major, we will find His peace becoming ours more and more as we experience His love and dish it out to others a day at a time and an act at a time. Love is righteous action to meet the needs of others, and when we pursue that, we are choosing a God-pleasing way of life.

You don't pursue emotions. You pursue things that you can do. You pursue actions of love.

Pursue love. Pursue agape.

On our refrigerator at home is the little slogan, "Choose joy."

We choose our emotions. We choose our actions. And someday we will be accountable for all that we've thought and done.

And so God says, through Paul, "Choose love." Follow after it. Make it your own.

It's so hard to run or jog when you don't know the goal.

Even if your goal is twelve minutes of strenuous activity a day, you have something to shoot for when at the seven-minute point, you are ready to quit. Anyone can go five more minutes.

I often say at the five-mile mark of a 10K race (6.2 miles), "Anybody can run one mile." Believe me, I can't wait to say that.

And it's probably true that anybody can run one mile, all things considered.

Anybody can take one more step.

And that is really how we run after love. We take another step. We go another mile. We help another person. We say just a few words in love.

It's not a matter of a dynamite explosion of love that changes your whole world overnight. I guess there have been those experiences. Conversion is that way in a sense. But most of growing in love is taking another step and stretching a little more and letting maturity and the Spirit of God at once become your strength.

That I can do. I can control my temper for just a few minutes more.

I can sit down and read just a few verses and pray a bit even though I don't feel like it.

I can lean over backwards for my teenager even though she isn't doing the same for me.

I can finish cleaning the garage for my wife, even though I really didn't feel like it in the first place.

Run after love. Don't give up. Don't let the greatness of the goal keep you from progress.

No one does that when it comes to health! No one thinks, "I'd like to be half healthy or I'd like to have just some of my organs working right."

We all want perfect health. And even though we all know we can't have totally perfect health, still we can pursue it. We can go another step. We can keep trying.

That's the way with perfect love. That's the way with total maturity. That's the way with whole commitment.

The fact is, when we pursue love we pursue God, because God is love. To have His kind of love in life, we must get to know Him. We must ask His strength. We must seek His Spirit. We must consciously say, "I am going to run toward God."

I am going to be what He wants me to be.

I am not going to listen to my feelings or to my lusts, but to my Lord. I'm going to do what my faith believes.

The closer we get to Him, the more of His love we're going to show.

Drawing closer to Christ. That's a stretching goal. It's not something that we ought to be haphazard about. It's a whole way of leaning over backwards to be something we're not naturally. It's asking God to give us a different approach to life, for His pleasure and glory.

I really believe it can happen. Because we are made in the image of God, we are made to reflect His glory. We do that in a special way when we love.

We reflect His image or mirror His goodness when we obey and stand in a loving, obedient relationship. Knowing that to be true, here is a prayer I often pray:

> Lord, You know my nature. I like myself and I'm willing to do things just for me. But I commit myself to love You. And because of that, to love others.
>
> Give me the grace to show that love daily. Help

me, with wisdom, to choose the way that would be best for others, to love them above myself.

Give me the strength to live for things that last, to care about others because You do, to be by Your Holy Spirit what I am not on my own.

We can do it together. I commit myself to run after love for the rest of my life. I ask You to help me gain on my goal, a little bit each day. Help me to walk in Your Spirit, whose fruit is love. Help me to follow Your Son, who was known as love.

I thank You. I love You.

When you pray a prayer like that, God hears. And He will answer.

Runners encourage each other all the time. Sometimes it's the solicited, "Tell me I can do it," or sometimes it's just a pat on the rump.

But it's brother helping brother.

Veteran pro athletes will often walk over to the nervous rookie and say something—perhaps a rebuke that's clearly picked up on the camera, but other times just a gentle word that probably translates, "We're with you, friend."

Let it be so among believers.

Let runners who band together in the spiritual running club we call the church be characterized by their willingness to pick each other up and help each other along. When one is overtaken in a fault, let the others go to the rescue, not to the phones.

Let people who are willing to run after Christ be willing to admit they need each other as well as Christ. Let them call a word of encouragement when there is a spiritual shin splint.

Let them share the water.

Let them pray together as they run, talk together as they go. And enjoy the beauty of camaraderie.

I can't always spell the word, but I know what it means.

I know what it means to be in a church where you trust your friends. Where loyalty is cherished. Where, if you have a cause or an offense against a brother, you go to that brother as Jesus prescribed in Matthew 18.

I know what it's like to see the opposite too. I have seen Christian runners kick and spike each other.

I have seen lead runners, whom we call elders or deacons, break the rules about gossip and tear apart the body of Christ.

And it is as if none of us cares that He died for our sins and rose again for our power.

The race is on and the runners are going. And we have so much going for us, especially Christ and His Spirit which unites.

Let the runners run together and with hope and encouragement for each other.

I love what Paul writes in Galatians 3:28: "There is neither Jew nor Greek, there is neither slave nor free man, there is neither male nor female; for you are all one in Christ Jesus."

Christianity is for all. While we are prone to make more of presidents than of street-cleaners and more of men than of women, we know that Christ did not. While He trained men to be spiritual leaders in the church and in the home, He called everyone to follow Him. And women can run with strength in ministry too. Their part is so very special in the church, whatever the church says about the pulpit. Our church does not allow for women to lead as pastors, and I am in agreement with that because I think Paul was.

But it certainly would die without the women's ministry.

"Member-ministers" we call them. If I had my way, we might add, "and runners."

But I won't push the analogy too often. Not everyone likes to talk about sports or running.

But everyone should like to talk about ministry. And

every man and woman, boy and girl has a part—if only each would realize it.

The process of human maturity is really the process of learning that we are not here on this earth for ourselves; we are here to run for Christ and then to help each other.

Most people, admittedly and sorrowfully, never learn the lesson.

And they die in their sins.

And even as Christians, many of us never really come alive because we never think beyond ourselves.

"God bless us four, no more"—the prayer of the family that is turned inward.

"Me, myself, and I"—the prayer of the individual who has never learned to give.

But such an attitude can be changed. Such is not life as Christ means it to be. The filling of the Spirit and the control of God comes to those who are willing to walk in the ways of Scripture, to do what is right, to live by faith, not by feelings.

I am sick and tired—I chose my words carefully—of those who talk about the filling of the Spirit or walking in the Spirit as something rather mystical, or as something reserved for church services or miracles or grand experiences.

The filling of the Spirit is for preaching, but it is also for daily living. For loving your wife. For honoring your husband. For obeying your parents.

Read the context about Spirit control and Word control in Ephesians 5:18 and Colossians 3:16 respectively, and you will see things that are as practical as night and day. As daily as sharing things at home or giving love on the phone or working hard where you work or paying your employees enough money.

That's what real running is.

That's the race called Christianity. That's the day-to-day stuff. Which leads to week-to-week, month-to-month, and right on into eternity.

That's the stuff of which Jesus said, "Well done, thou good and faithful servant" (Matt. 25:21, KJV).

Cups of cold water given in His name.

Prisoners visited in His name.

Floors scrubbed in His name.

Screws turned in His name at General Motors.

Brains operated on in His name at Mayo Clinic.

Children loved in His name.

And it's not that you name His name every time, but that your life is for His glory and He knows that and feels it because you do. Your run is for His pleasure.

Joe Henderson, the running editor of *Runner's World* magazine, said, "I write, because the thoughts inside have to be put in more visible form. I run, because it's inside pushing to get out."

Maybe that's true for the best of runners.

For sure, it's true that something inside us is pushing for eternity. Solomon writes, "[God] has also set eternity in the hearts of men" (Ecc. 3:11, NIV). Something deep within us wants to be connected to God.

We need to be more than just beings who eat, sleep, and get up to eat and sleep again.

We throw in some work. And play.

But it's still not enough. There is more.

Remember the climax of *Chariots of Fire?* Eric Liddell and Harold Abrams both won gold medals for Britain in the 1924 Olympics. Liddell ran for God's glory, and laughed with joy as friends hoisted him onto their shoulders to celebrate the victory.

Harold Abrams ran for Harold Abrams. After the race, he sat with his coach, Sam Mussobini, at a Paris sidewalk cafe, sipping beer. Very depressed, Abrams did not know how to handle his victory.

Coach Mussobini says, "The whole world can go to hell, Harold. Tell them you run for you and old Sam Mussobini.

That's all that matters."

As the camera pans back, Abrams, unconvinced, sipped his beer once more.

Eric Liddell was full. Harold Abrams was empty. And the truth—God's truth—is never clearer: there is so much more to live for than just self.

Run after love!

9

FOCUSING AS YOU RUN

"Therefore, since we have so great a cloud of witnesses surrounding us, let us also lay aside every encumbrance, and the sin which so easily entangles us, and let us run with endurance the race that is set before us, fixing our eyes on Jesus, the author and perfecter of faith, who for the joy set before Him endured the cross, despising the shame, and has sat down at the right hand of the throne of God."
(Heb. 12:1-2)

"For you have been called for this purpose, since Christ also suffered for you, leaving you an example for you to follow in His steps."
(1 Peter 2:21)

We all blow it so easily. We are made to learn, and we get mad because there's school.

We're made to worship, and we wonder why Sunday comes around so quickly, or who cares about morning devotions.

We were made to love; instead we claw.

It's our fault. God made a beautiful world and we messed it up. Solomon says it so well: "God made mankind upright, but men have gone in search of many schemes" (Ecc. 7:29, NIV).

We pay to go to college and then pray for snow days.

We pay fabulous sums to join exercise clubs, drive luxurious cars to and from, and buy doughnuts or ice cream on the way home afterward.

We are people of contradictions and we might as well admit it, then plug into principles that really help us conquer our sinful tendencies in the name of Christ.

First, we must realize that we were made to know God, to love Him, to obey Him, and to find our greatest fulfillment in doing His wishes—which include enjoying all the things that He has given us! First Timothy 6:10-11 doesn't tell a rich man to relinquish all his wealth, but it does advise him to enjoy the riches and recognize that it is God who has given them to him.

It's God who says, "Enjoy life with your wife" (Ecc. 9:9, NIV).

He is no spoilsport in the heavens seeking to slap our hands. He made us with good reason and for good reasons.

But instead, we try not to learn; we eat too much; we play with sex instead of using it for His glory and for His kind of joy.

We blow it.

And if we admit that, we're on the first step toward getting back to where we need to be, as best we can by the grace of God.

Then we may be ready to fix our eyes on Christ, to stare at His goodness and receive His grace!

This is the good fix.

This is the one stare that is really healthy.

"Fixing our eyes on Jesus, the author and perfecter of faith," is the command for all spiritual runners. It's Hebrews 12:1-2 that tells us to run with endurance, and it's verse 2 especially that tells us how we're going to keep going even when it's rough.

Not by looking at our teachers, though they are to be our examples.

Not by just watching our parents, though their lives should be an inspiration.

Not by simply noting the faith of fellow Christians and following our spiritual leaders, though we are commanded by God to do that.

We are to turn our eyes to Jesus Christ.

We can't help but watch each other. That's why we have stars. We like to read about people who hit the long ball, write bestsellers, and win Academy Awards.

Similarly, we like to elevate spiritual heroes to the Christian limelight.

I guess some of that is OK. But much of it is devastating, because those pillars often fall. And when they do, the people watching them sometimes go down too.

Hebrews 13 teaches, "Remember those who led you, who spoke the Word of God to you; and considering the result of their conduct, imitate their faith" (v. 7).

Clearly, spiritual leadership should keep that truth in mind.

But verse 8 throws in a caution: "Jesus Christ is the same yesterday and today, yes and forever."

He is the one to watch!

Look what He did! He is something else!

He began our faith and finished it. He's the one who

cried out from the cross, "It is finished."

Early in His life He set His face to do the Father's will and to author our salvation. Even as a child He grew "in wisdom and stature, and in favor with God and men" (Luke 2:52). He had His rough days, I'm sure. But He never had a sinful day.

He endured the shame and made it. And according to Hebrews 12:2, He is now sitting "at the right hand of the throne of God."

Not that there is an actual throne room with three thrones—God the Father in the middle, Christ on the right hand, and the Holy Spirit on the left or else doing the messenger service. Being at the right hand of the throne of God symbolizes two major truths about the Lord Jesus:

1. *His authority*. Christ is the right hand of God. It's a little bit like the lesser idea, "He's my right-hand man." Jesus sits at that place of authority.

Remember the time when the mother of James and John, like the Little League mother who screams for her child, wanted her two sons to sit "on the right hand and on the left hand" of Jesus? She was in essence asking for places of dignity and authority for her boys.

2. *His finished act of atonement*. Christ's work in making salvation possible was accomplished. He sat down.

Unlike the high priest who never got to sit down in the sense of accomplishing his annual duty or his daily chores as a priest, Jesus sat down. His job was finished.

He would not have to do that again.

"Once for all" He died for our sins (1 Peter 3:18).

Now we can look at Him, knowing that the job is finished. We don't have to worry about it.

I don't have to do anything today to get in with God. I don't have to earn anything. I can't. It's impossible!

Righteousness before a holy God staggers me. Without the blood of Christ, how in the world could I walk up to Him and say that I'm ready to have my interview for admission to heaven. No way.

I should look at Jesus Christ and know that what He did totally fulfilled the plan of God. He is the *propitiation*, a word I can hardly say. But I can surely smile about it. It means that God is totally satisfied. The work of salvation is completed.

I can look at Jesus and keep on running out of sheer gratitude because my standing is already settled before God.

I am running because I'm already loved, not to get loved. I'm running for Christ because I'm already accepted, not hoping to be accepted.

I'm enduring because I know He cares enough to have paid the price for sin.

Remember when you were little and picked sides for neighborhood softball games. In our neighborhood, Clint was always chosen first, Gardner second, and I usually was picked third or fourth (that's not real spectacular if you know that there were only five on a side!).

Finally the selection process came down to the last two guys—a chubby one and a weak hitter.

Leftovers.

I am so glad to announce that God does not see any of us that way. He likes difference. He doesn't think brawn or brains is most important. He loves us in a special way—and individually.

You might feel like you're standing around waiting for God to pick you. Let me tell you a wonderful message: Christ died for you and wants you to be part of His family.

So as you run, focus on Christ. Focus on His finished work.

Focus on His example also.

When I was little, my father would often say, "Don't do as I do; do as I say."

He meant it as a joke, but also as an admission of some failures on his part.

Jesus says both: "Do as I do; do as I say."

And when we do, we experience life at its fullest satisfaction. We become what God means for us to be. We can obey Him and keep running.

It's really good exercise to sit down and read the life of Jesus Christ in the Gospels. Sometimes we can become discouraged seeing all the frail children of dust around us, ourselves included. A look at Jesus will provide renewed joy and hope.

He loved people of all kinds, shapes, and sizes. He didn't have to say much about it—He was forever showing it—but He taught about that love too. "I did not come to call the righteous, but sinners" (Matt. 9:13).

He told people to love their neighbors, anyone around them, just like they loved themselves (Luke 10:27). And even though His own neighbors rejected Him, yet He loved them. He took time with them.

Children would run to sit on His lap. The lepers had a saying among themselves: "Jesus is one of us." The crippled had hearts that skipped a beat when they saw Him coming. Even when they were not among the ones He healed, He brought courage into their souls. It was not the magic He brought to their muscles—it was the way He touched and talked to them. It was the tenderness they felt in His calloused hands.

Yes, Jesus loves us. It's one of the first songs we learn by heart, and it strengthens our hearts still.

He befriended the herpes carriers, without a thought of falling. He sat down with winebibbers, but never made a selfish or foolish move. He moved toward people others ran away from. He allowed a streetwalker to wash His feet with her tears, dry them with her hair, and walk quietly away with newfound forgiveness and peace in her heart. "The tax-gatherers and harlots did believe Him" (Matt. 21:32).

Friend of sinners, He came for me. Associate of the selfish, He went to the house of Zaccheus for tea, and ended up at mine.

For I was that sinner, and I that crippled fool. I was covered with the leprosy of selfishness and He did not run away, but held my hand.

I was a child of hell, but He adopted me and reassigned my eternity.

I was a mixed-up teenager with pimples on my face and questions on my soul and He taught me how to live.

He lifted me, and for no reason. No, for one reason—love!

Nothing displays His supernatural grace and love like His reaction to those who despised Him. He did not get even, but left that up to His Heavenly Father, as should we.

They asked trick questions. He answered graciously, but pointedly. If they were hurting someone else, He stepped in, and stuck their feet in their mouths, as at the time when the hypocritical Pharisees were about to execute a woman caught in immorality. But when it would have been personal revenge, He opened not His mouth.

"Love your enemies," He taught in the Sermon on the Mount. "Return good for evil." "When someone slaps you on your cheek, turn to him your other."

And then He got the chance to practice what He preached. They slapped Him on the face, and He prayed for them. They gouged His eyes, and He cried for them.

He was tied to a slab and whipped on the back in the vicious Roman manner, and He endured with patience.

They pulled out His beard whiskers with wooden pliers and He did not call down angels to the rescue.

They (in a sense, we were all there) got a crowd to sway from its Palm Sunday admiration and call for His death, all the time mocking His lack of power to stop the sideshow.

They laughed at His "weakness," as they labeled it, and smashed thorns deeply into His throbbing forehead. They spit in His face, yet He remained calm.

They put Him through the mockery of a trial, fixed and fraudulent, and He endured. "Thou sayest," He said when asked if He was God, admitting He was truth.

They killed Him, not in a quick extermination, but in the cruelest and most humiliating of tortures, "even the death on the cross." He would leave a cup of juice and a piece of bread so we would never forget.

He was marched through the alleyways of Jerusalem as an exhibit of Roman victory. Carrying a heavy cross, He was whipped again.

They say the beauty of a man's character comes out under pressure. Here were all the physical, emotional, mental, social, and spiritual forces pushing against one Person all alone, and His character was only holy, His response only loving.

His enemies hammered spikes into His wrists and ankles, and hung Him, naked, to an upright cross, where He was jeered by the soldiers and the crowd.

He only responded, "Father, forgive them—they know not what they do."

In the hell He faced, He showed that He is heaven.

When I am maligned, I picture His reactions to the people's gossip and cruelty, and I gain new strength.

I can endure. He did.

He runs with me in the quiet morning hours, when I look out above my shoulder and see the stars still out and know that He, their maker, does not sleep.

He runs with me in the beauty of a spring morning when the sun is whispering that it will be hot and the grass is smelling like a friend that calls you to come lie down and gaze at the clouds. I sense His beautiful creativity, and know that His design is even for my life.

He has run with me in the hard days of marriage, those days when I was selfish or when some schedule or invading force from outside had hurt our electricity, and Jeanine and I were not on common ground. We have made the commitment and He has come and pulled us back together by the grace of forgiveness, and we have run as three.

He has run with me in those weakest of moments, when I have faced death with desolation, reeling from the tragedies of my own sister and mother, or someone very special in the church whose love for Christ was so strong, but whose daughter was hit by the drunken driver.

Progress seems to be the most important product all through the Scriptures. The Bible clearly demonstrates there is no such thing as instant maturity, but Christian growth is called for over and over again. "Grow in grace and in the knowledge of our Lord and Saviour Jesus Christ" (2 Peter 3:18) typifies commands to Christians, and is a cover-all for a lot of specific commands about that growth.

The New Testament epistles were written to churches where people had become Christians but now needed to know how to treat each other, how to have godly marriages, how to react when someone really got their tempers to explode. Indeed, so much of the content of the New Testament is the pattern for growth, giving maps and compasses for our daily lives.

In that sense, it is very much a run—with progress plotted a step at a time. We are not at the finish line the first day we accept Christ.

That day of decision is a starting line. The gun goes off, and we are saved. We are forgiven. Justification is a matter of being made righteous before God by His declaration, and on account of the holy righteousness of Jesus Christ Himself. He covers us with His goodness, giving us the gift of righteousness as He forgives our sins.

The exchange is more than wonderful!

This is salvation.

But the Christian run proceeds from that point till the day we die. It requires that we follow Christ in our lives. We go by the Word. We listen to His commands. And we move forward.

People invent all kinds of shortcuts, and come back from their various "experiences of God" with news that they have made it, but they too have to take another step at a time and walk each day in the grace of Christ.

I ought to be loving my wife more this year than last year. I ought to be knowing the Lord better now than I did five years ago, and rejoicing in Him more, and learning to give thanks more generously, and handling differences with others better. That is progress and growth.

It is the Spirit's fruit in my life.

But there will be more. I need to keep growing. I can't stop here and just thank Him for what has happened.

The runner doesn't stop halfway through the race and clap because he is ahead of someone! He keeps running. His destiny is the finish line, not just progress.

That's why Paul says, "Not that I have already attained," and vows that he will keep on going.

He turns around as he runs and urges all of us to follow.

When a person is sick, nothing seems right. Take some time if you feel good today to notice how good it feels to feel good.

Relish it. Celebrate it.

And then the next time you feel bad, you'll be able to endure a little better.

The same is true spiritually. When a person is not focusing on or walking with the Lord—running, if you please—nothing else will seem right. When you are out of step with Christ, you are unable to take someone's offense properly. Enemies appear to be Goliaths instead of just normal human beings who made a mistake.

Such is sickness. Such is life. And healing comes only when we walk with the Lord. Then we can even love our enemies.

Howard Hendricks loves to tell the story of the man who said he couldn't love his wife. The marriage counselor told him he should at least love her as his neighbor since they were living together.

"I don't even want to live near her and I can't call her a neighbor," replied the husband.

"Then," said the counselor with a bit of desperation, "love her as an enemy!"

I was catching up on a little relaxation and watching the Van Cliburn world's amateur piano contest several years ago. As the program was going off the air and the winner, Steven DeGroote, was playing a very strong and difficult classical piece, you could hear his taped words: "If you want to give yourself to music, you must never think of the rewards. Think only of the music. Never look back. Think always, 'If I were not in music, there is nothing else!' "

I had just been studying the endurance passage in Hebrews 12, so that Sunday I let Steven DeGroote help Paul and me with the sermon.

If I want to keep going in life, and endure, and "remain under" the disciplines or the pain, I must realize that there really is nothing but Christ.

Everything else must line up under that, but He is the main attraction. All things were made by Him and for Him. Without Him was not anything made that was made (Col. 1:16-17).

If I focus on Him, I will buffet my body. I will keep on running. I will not give up. I will not lose heart.

I will endure another minute and another hour and another day and another week and another month and another year and another ten years until He comes.

But I must focus on Him.

And then when He comes, I will "love His appearing," as Paul says everyone should do who wants to be rewarded.

So, oversimplified, it all does come down to a relationship with Christ and realizing who He is and what He has promised. Believing Him.

Having faith.

Running with that in mind.

With Him in mind.

Then you can endure.

Otherwise, you will cop out or drop out or slop out.

People do it all the time.

In Richard Bach's classic tale *Jonathan Livingston Seagull*, the father of the gull reminded his son, "Don't you forget that the reason you fly is to eat."

Jonathan had wanted to go higher than ever before, with precision, speed, and endurance. But his family was trying to talk him out of it, encouraging him to focus on the goal.

The reason we live is to eat, many say. "Meat is for the belly, and the belly is for meat."

But as believers we know the reason we live is much higher than that. It is to do one thing—to glorify God and to know His Son, Jesus Christ.

He is the Lord and should be central, the focus of our eyes, the object of our love, the source of our truth.

Forget the other things and let this be your passion!

Focus!

10

GOOD NEWS FOR WEAK KNEES

"Therefore, strengthen the hands that are weak and the knees that are feeble."

(Heb. 12:12)

Sports have so many great parallels for the Christian life. And individuals exemplify many of the principles of self-denial and discipline that we are talking about here.

Great football coaches like Knute Rockne and Vince Lombardi—great in that order, of course—virtually taught people how to play above their limits.

Knute Rockne's biography tells of the day he revved up his troops so much at an away game that they went out the wrong door from the dressing room, and the first three fell into the swimming pool.

They were hot. They were high. High on Rockne.

He put heart into them!

Lombardi had that same power to ignite. And, of course, so do many other coaches in all sports at every level.

The job of the pastor on Sunday is not totally unlike that of the coach. But then the "game" is when the "players" leave the church.

That's where we live our faith. That's where we run the race.

The race is not on Sundays at the church building, but on Monday through Saturday at the home and at the office and at the police station and in the car and on the crowded freeways and in the company cafeteria and in the neighborhood.

I once saw the ad in a runners' magazine that announced: "Good news for weak knees."

I have weak knees. Too often.

I'll be plodding along at a decent clip for a mediocre runner, and all of a sudden, it seems, my right knee is hurting again.

"An old football injury," I like to say when I have to explain it. Actually, my football experience in high school yielded no such lasting trophies. I could wish.

But, of course, the weakness did not come all of a sudden. It developed.

Such are most of our weaknesses for running the Christian race. They certainly do not surge into our spirits on a moment's notice. They build. They *become* our weaknesses. They linger.

We allow them.

And they hold us back as a result.

But now there is good news for weak knees—and this is for all of us!

There is a cure!

We can be helped.

Like the pain, the cure may take time. It will not be just a shot we need. Long-term therapy is called for.

But help is available.

Sometimes knowing that is really all we need to get into the prescription.

The runner in Hebrews gives clear instructions: "Strengthen the hands that are weak and the knees that are feeble, and make straight paths for your feet, so that the limb which is lame may not be put out of joint, but rather be healed" (Heb. 12:12-13).

That clear command is in a context about discipline. Many runners fade or faint when they experience discipline or testing in their lives as God's children. Soft we all are, and a healthy test from God in the form of discipline from the Father is meant to strengthen us.

Instead, we often refuse to learn the lesson of discipline and have to go through life with the pain, but not the good it was meant to bring.

"He disciplines us for our good, that we may share His holiness" (Heb. 12:10). He disciplines us to strengthen our weak knees, not to hurt us.

When we learn from our failures, and grow through our sorrows, we are "trained," to use God's word, by the pain. As the saying goes, "No pain, no gain." We need hard times to grow by, to make us see our inadequacies and weaknesses.

We tend to become spoiled brats spiritually unless we face hard times. And spoiled brats need to be spanked! So, for two reasons a hard time can be very healthy for us!

One, it can do wonders for our knees, our weak knees.

And two, it can discipline us for disobedience.

A good physical runner takes care of his knees and feet. He doesn't panic when he feels a pain or new sensation, but neither does he push his luck. He knows how vital his knees are for a good run!

The good news in the spiritual realm is that God wants us to have strong knees and a healthy run in this life. He is a loving Father who does not care to let us wander on our own. He will discipline through setbacks, a physical reprimand, or a colleague's criticism.

If we are willing to learn the lesson out of the discipline and correct the selfishness or sin of the situation, we can have our knees strengthened.

This is the good news.

Which builds good knees.

Which help us run better, for His glory!

So the writer of Hebrews smiles, finally, about God's fatherly discipline and concludes, "To those who have been trained by it, afterwards it yields the peaceful fruit of righteousness" (Heb. 12:11).

Righteous knees run better.

In a nutshell, the best way to react to pain or a setback shows a sequence:

1. *Thank God He is still Lord.* "Give thanks in all circumstances" (1 Thes. 5:18, NIV).

2. *Consider any way out of the pain that would be better for you.* I am not among the breed of Christian masochists who speak as if they enjoy pain. Even Jesus prayed, "If it is possible, let this cup [of suffering] pass from Me" (Matt. 26:39).

3. *Be sure to consider if the pain or problem could be*

loving discipline from God. If you have been hanging on to sin in some area, let go. Be healed and forgiven.

James 5:14-16 very explicitly shows how a helpless condition can be brought on by continued sin.

4. *If you get only negative answers to steps 2 and 3, pray for relief.* In other words, accept your situation. Here is your opportunity to be strong in weakness.

Now clearly, sometimes weak knees are not direct disciplines from God, but are the natural consequences of losing heart, of our failure to run our lives the way God wishes or wills.

To lose heart is to faint, or to get weak-kneed, or crushed beneath the load.

To lose momentum.

I'm sure you have watched your favorite football team do it at times. Ahead and looking unstoppable, gradually the other team or some invisible force eats the heart out of them and they lose drive and soul.

They are done unless a turnaround takes place.

Heart is a big factor in any contest of life. We watch the raging forces around young Daniel, and we see that he "purposed in his heart" (Dan. 1:8, KJV) to do what was right. To not eat what he should not eat. To stick with the disciplines of righteousness.

We are what we will and decide in our hearts, and it shows in our attitudes and actions.

A man with a big heart, large with love and obedience, can go a long way for God.

The New Testament outlines six ways that God helps us avoid loss of heart! Now to be sure, He does not list all these in a single paragraph under the heading, "The following are the ways people lose heart." But the phrase does crop up throughout the Gospels and epistles and makes for interesting study.

1. *We lose heart by quitting prayer.* Jesus says in essence, "Men ought always to pray and not lose heart" (Luke 18:1).

So teaching, He implies that the opposite of not continuing to pray is losing heart.

And with the world we live in and all the spiritual failures we witness around us, it's not hard to see that if we don't pray, stay in close touch with God, and seek His strength, we're going to lose heart.

Like a football team in the third quarter. They call on their star halfback again and again, but he doesn't gain any yardage. And so the quarterback quits calling the halfback's number and the team inwardly gives up. They lose heart.

Jesus follows His instruction with the parable of a woman who kept knocking on the door of the town judge, asking for justice.

In fact, she became a real pest with her pounding—to the point that the judge granted her request.

The woman didn't quit, and that's the whole point of the story.

Don't quit when you start to pray for something. If you nonchalantly pray, or mention your request only in a passing conversation with God, you haven't really *prayed* for it! To pray is to seek, to knock, to ask. To be overly persistent.

In other words, keep at it if you really want it.

Don't lose heart.

I was in my early twenties when a close friend of our family asked me, "What's the use of praying? God's going to do what He wants to anyway."

At that point in her life, this friend was ready to stop praying.

I felt the same way. She had stood with us through the tragic death of my sister at fourteen. And this was the day of my mother's funeral, my mother, who was dead at age forty-six.

This friend and I had prayed intensely for both.

I was at church when I got the call that my sister had fallen off a horse, hit her head on a rock, and was in a coma.

A few years later, and never fully recovered from the loss of my sister, my mother had died young.

Why keep praying if "bad" things happen anyway?

I say all that to say it began several years of hard struggle for me on that question. I'm still not a very good pray-er, but this diagram helps me keep at it:

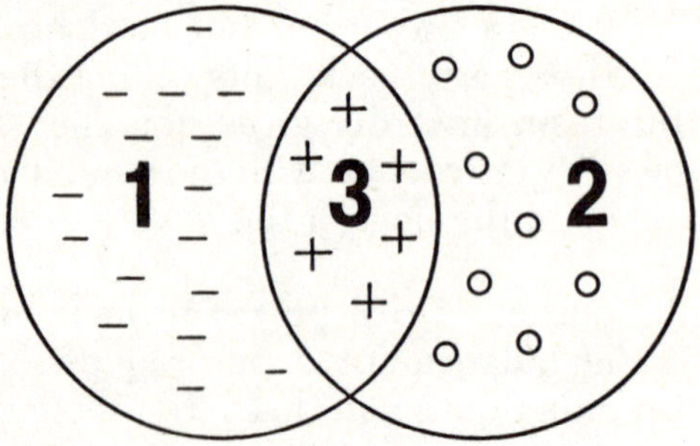

Oversimplifying, let's say there are three categories of prayer requests or circumstances.

#1 refers to things that we ask for, but do not get.

#2 includes things that God would give us if we prayed.

#3 includes all answered prayers.

Whenever the two circles cross, it indicates we're asking for things that God wills for us . . . and there is answered prayer.

It's like the two circles in the middle of my 35mm camera. Whenever those two circles come together, the picture is in focus. I can show you a lot of slides where the circles weren't overlapping!

Referring to #1, James says that there are some things we do not have because we are asking "with wrong motives" (James 4:3)—a rather blunt way of saying that we just want it because we want it because we want it.

As when a two-year-old asks for more candy.

Category #2 includes those things that James refers to when he says, "You do not have because you do not ask" (James 4:2). Apparently, God has a supply of things that He would like to do in our lives, but in His sovereignty He waits until we pray.

God doesn't lose any power in this plan, but He does say some of His work depends on our prayers.

Category #3 includes all those things that come under the heading, "Ask in Jesus' name." More than just tacking on those words at the end of the prayer, it means asking in the will of Christ and seeking to do His glory and pleasure.

That's the essence of my diagram, which helps me keep praying, not fainting.

Paul says that we should "pray always." Never quit. That's 1 Thessalonians 5:18.

That's something like saying, "Never quit eating." It doesn't mean that you're eating all the time, but that you keep it as a regular part of your life.

Praying should be a regular part of each day, part of our spiritual breathing with the Lord.

If we quit, we will become faint-hearted. We'll live on our own and act on our own, and we really can't make it that way in this earthly atmosphere.

I know what it's like to stop praying. I have at times. Probably you have too. Far too many Christians do not pray anymore. Oh, maybe a quick grace or "gracette" at each meal or snack, but little in terms of real conversation or communication.

Hearts faint when they stop praying.

2. *We lose heart in the spiritual run when we forget what grace is and latch on to legalism.* Paul says, "Since we have . . . received such mercy, we do not lose heart" (2 Cor. 4:1).

It is mercy that helps us keep going.

If I thought that my standing with God today were based on what I do today, and that He was checking me out and comparing me with Christ and deciding if He still loved me, I would lose heart.

My heart is depraved. I say dumb things or think wrong thoughts all the time.

I don't mean all the time, but I mean frequently.

Christ knows everything about me.

But I have a ministry of mercy. I can tell myself that Christ died for my sins and be clean in Christ. Forgiven by His blood.

I have a ministry of mercy to preach from a pulpit and in my neighborhood. Christ Jesus died for our sins, yours and mine, and God sees us as "accepted in the Beloved," a place of great security and grace.

Since we know that kind of grace, we need not lose heart.

It's also in this passage that Paul says his great theme is to "preach not ourselves, but Christ Jesus the Lord; and ourselves your servants for Jesus' sake" (2 Cor. 4:5).

That's different from preaching what we have to do to get in with God. Sure, we're servants. Sure, we commit ourselves to others.

But all because of grace.

I'm convinced that many Christians do not understand what grace really means. They add oil to water or legalism to grace and talk about being accepted by Christ but also doing the best they can to stay in with the Lord.

"Well, I accepted Christ when I was twelve and I've always tried to do the best I can since then," the person replies.

Or the famous: "I was baptized by ________"—then they name their favorite preacher.

Or, "I went forward when I was seven."

Congratulations!

But grace is related to what Christ did for us and when we were identified with Him by faith.

I don't think God is listening to the way we say it, but where the object of our faith is.

That's the issue. And when the object of our faith is the grace of Christ, we can feel secure. He wants us to, in fact!

Otherwise, we are going to lose heart.

My theory is that all legalists either lose heart and drop out or get bitter!

I've known a lot of both!

Majoring on grace and what God has done for me and how He sees me through the righteousness of Christ, according to Romans 3–5, is what keeps me running, anyway!

3. *We lose heart by losing hope.* Second Corinthians 4:16 talks clearly about this: "Therefore, we do not lose heart, but though our outer man is decaying, yet our inner man is being renewed day by day."

Without thoughts of the future and the hope of eternal life and the day of great correction, we all will lose heart.

That's why many people drop out of the Christian race, or seem to, when they look at what others are getting away with. Christian teens can't understand why some kids at the high school who mock Christ also get elected "Most Popular." Christian businessmen can't understand why fellow workers who lie, cheat, and steal make their way up the corporate ladder.

Paul is very realistic when he brings up how his outer man is going downhill.

I think that happens right after age twenty-eight. At least, some say that's the peak of an individual's running or athletic prowess, and that it's all downhill after that.

Paul knew physical disability. He also knew suffering due to discrimination and persecution. He knew that his outer man was decaying.

But his inner man was getting stronger as he went!

And all because he had such hope of seeing Christ and being with Him. All the great symbolic truths of 2 Corinthians 5, when we leave this tent behind and get the brand-new tent and the glorified state of being with Christ . . . all of that is a reminder of the "blessed hope" we have.

And that keeps us from losing heart.

If I thought that everything was wrapped up with this life, and that death was the final event, I would not work nearly as hard in the church.

In fact, I would probably drop out, give up my beliefs, and concentrate on eating, drinking, and being merry.

I think that's what Paul would have done, if I read him right in 1 Corinthians 15:32.

Instead, Paul tells us to work hard! He says that no work is in vain or empty (1 Cor. 15:58).

And that great verse follows a whole chapter about resurrection and the hope we have for tomorrow.

When the psalmist cries out with joy: "My heart overflows with a good theme" (Ps. 45:1), it is because he has found the King and he knows the future.

We have great hope about tomorrow.

Maybe it's "pie in the sky" to some.

Personally, I like pie, wherever I get it!

And I can have a little bit of it right now when I see the glory of God and how He makes things work together for good and supplies grace and answers to prayer.

But some things remain in the realm of hope, not present reality.

Things described in John's Revelation not here yet, but sure nonetheless.

One day we will be with Christ!

Knowing that keeps me running.

As in so many things, balance is key here. Memories and gratitude for heritage are essential.

But *hope* is a great word to God. He gives it to us. He

lets us use it because of His grace. So we can run knowing we can finish. Knowing that at the finish line, it will be very good.

Look ahead. Look to Jesus. Check His future plans.

Run with endurance.

4. *We lose heart when we become tired or burned out.* A lot of books talk about this now as a new phenomenon. Paul wrote about the same condition in the first century when he said, "And let us not lose heart in doing good, for in due time we shall reap if we do not grow weary" (Gal. 6:9).

Many lose heart by just plain getting tired, giving up.

It does get old to do good, good, good.

Especially if people aren't rewarding you or thanking you or recognizing your labor in return.

As a pastor, I have often known of Sunday School teachers or other church volunteers who resigned their positions because "nobody ever thanked me."

Thanks is a great reward, and appreciation goes a long way to keep you going a long way!

Many lose heart because they work hard and don't see results right away.

Verses like Galatians 6:9 are included in Scripture to help us keep running.

To say to us, "Keep doing good, good, good, because you will eventually reap what you sow."

Sometimes in this life, sometimes in the next.

But you will get what's coming to you.

In due time!

God's time.

A farmer doesn't put the seed in the ground, start cheering, and then get disgusted and unearth it if the thing doesn't grow immediately. He waits. Galatians 6:9 tells us to act the same way.

It will come. It will come. It will come.

So do good. Do good. Do good. Do good.

Christ did.

We look around the church and see a lot of dropouts. It's the old 80-20 rule in operation. Eighty percent of the people do 20 percent of the work and 20 percent of the people do 80 percent of the work! The same rule applies when it comes to church giving.

Yes, some have dropped out; some have never even tried!

But keep running! You will reap what you sow. No cup of cold water given in Jesus' name goes unnoticed.

I like that. I can keep running when I remember that.

I need to see doing good in that same light.

I remember when one of our daughters was rather small and she came around the corner of the kitchen/dining room combination and saw Jeanine and me hugging and kissing.

One of the privileges of marriage.

"Gross out," was her contemporary reply.

She has since changed her mind.

And doing good may seem a waste to many young Christians, especially when they see little in terms of results or appreciation at times.

But it is the stuff that Christ was made of. And it can be ours in a special way.

Don't lose heart. Christ will reward. Keep trusting Him!

One thing I like about physical running is that you do it alone. Now, I am not by nature a loner. And yet, like all men, I am in a way. One of the great tests of life is how you like it when you're by yourself.

If you pass that test, you'll be able to spend time with others with good success.

Running makes you free of dependence and lets you look at your own likes and willpower and lungs. Like wrestling, there's just you and the other.

The other, in the case of running, is the enemy. Not the

hill. Not the lack of water. The enemy is you. "We have located the enemy and it is us," said Pogo of cartoon fame.

And the Apostle Paul agrees in Romans 7, when he says how frustrated he is with the battle that wages inside him.

Running the Christian life lets us look truthfully at ourselves and then evaluate how we're going to relate to Christ. The first step toward that end is realizing how strong we can be on our own and yet how weak we are spiritually when we're strong on our own.

It's the great paradox. "When I am weak, then I am strong."

Or to turn it around and say it with just as much truth, "When I am strong, then I am weak."

Strong in self, that is. Strong in willpower. Strong in determination to do our own thing.

It's a fine line, but it's a very important one: when we submit to the lordship of Christ we find strength by being weak to selfishness.

That strength of heart can keep us going.

5. *We lose heart when we're tested.* Paul writes to the believers at Ephesus, "Therefore I ask you not to lose heart at my tribulations on your behalf, for they are your glory" (Eph. 3:13).

Many people cannot handle tribulation, even though Jesus promised it (John 16:33). It's easy to forget what God is doing in the world, and fool ourselves into thinking that He's here just to grow apples and pears and make everybody smile.

There are also weeds.

There are accidents. People shoot other people. Nations bomb nations. Cancer rips at our insides.

Don't lose heart, says Paul. This world is not our home, and these tests are allowed by God to help make gold out of stubble and to remind us that this life is a mere swamp when compared to the paradise of heaven.

Christians may actually face more tests than non-Christians! They have more areas to be tested in, including a whole list of beliefs and commitments that a non-Christian doesn't even have!

So it can be a strain.

But don't lose heart!

6. *We lose heart when we take our eyes off Jesus.* The writer to the Hebrews exhorts, "Consider Him who has endured such hostility by sinners against Himself, so that you may not grow weary and lose heart" (Heb. 12:3).

Run with endurance by looking at Christ.

The only reason anybody keeps praying or doing good or growing under tests, or preaching mercy instead of law, is by looking at Christ.

That comes with daily meetings with Him and regular worship, but also by focusing our minds.

Otherwise, we lose heart. If your eyes are only on some all-star Christian, you're going to find some faults. He'll talk about money too much on TV, or he'll run off with somebody's organist, or he'll simply age and say something rather senile.

Don't lose heart. Set your mind on Christ.

Such is the way to keep going.

Just as striking as watching a team lose heart and give momentum away is watching that same team get revved up by a big play or a turned-on crowd, and grab the momentum back again.

Sometimes a sub comes off the bench and puts the spark into the offense. A rally ensues.

It's exciting to watch, and even more thrilling to experience.

How's your heart?

11

GOOD NEWS FOR NON-RUNNERS

"Then the Lord answered me and said, 'Record the vision and inscribe it on tablets, that the one who reads it may run.

" 'For the vision is yet for the appointed time; it hastens toward the goal, and it will not fail. Though it tarries, wait for it; for it will certainly come, it will not delay.

" 'Behold, as for the proud one, his soul is not right within him; but the righteous will live by his faith.' "

(Hab. 2:2-4)

I really don't think everyone should be a runner or a jogger. But I do believe that everyone ought to get some kind of regular physical exercise, for arteriosclerosis is fast becoming a major health culprit in our society.

We need to clear up the clog in our veins and let the blood flow through better so we can function longer.

But I don't want to get into medicine or have to answer the fears of those who say you can hurt your knees if you jog too much.

I want to draw a parallel with spiritual running.

It's hard to try to explain the feeling of running or the aftermath, the point of feeling good and hungry and leaner and more "circulated"! People who have never jogged don't understand. I've been embarrassed a few times when I've tried to explain how I felt and then realized that I was talking with someone who had never felt that way and didn't seem to be interested. Usually I quit.

The same tension is there spiritually. Many people have not known the Lord through faith, have not sensed forgiveness in their lives or the purpose that Christ gives, have not had fellowship with Him. Even people who claim to know Christ often have stayed shallow or have never grown in their lives, and when we talk about our spiritual relationship with them, it's plain they'd rather be talking about something else.

God told the Prophet Habakkuk, "Write the vision plain, so that people can run" (Hab. 2:2, Larson paraphrase).

"Spell it out clearly, so that people can make progress in their lives and do what's right."

"State God's truth as it should be stated. Tell it so that even children can understand."

"And when the people really understand the message, they will be able to run the race."

That's a great command for pastors and teachers today. It stands as permanent for all of us: "Write the vision plain."

But exactly what truth does the vision contain?

First, the proud man is really sick, and the faithful man is really just (Hab. 2:4).

The whole Book of Habakkuk is about the huge question WHY? It is a monstrous question, twenty feet tall.

The people of Habakkuk's day were jealous of the proud, who seemed to have things going for them.

And some who were righteous were living in rags.

"Write the vision plain," God says. Speak it clearly. The proud people are going to stumble and fall when they look around and see the hard questions of life.

The heroes of the world are the athletes and the singers, many of whom appear godless.

Who makes all the money—the faithful factory worker or the unselfish missionary or the salesman with clean hands and a pure heart?

Not often. Often it's the guy who takes money under the table.

Or someone merchandising his body or his talents.

"But don't quit running," is the message of Habakkuk. God has an answer. God will bring judgment someday.

Even though the crops fail, God will make our running to be like the running of the hind, the beautiful deer that jumps on the mountaintops with joy (Hab. 3:19).

Even though the crops fail, the fruit trees don't blossom, and the calves don't return to their stalls—God will still care for His people. He will give them inner strength.

Those last verses of Habakkuk (3:17-19) strike a bell of hope and keep us running. They keep us doing what's right.

And so we need to share the message in a very clear and plain way.

"Write the vision plain!"

I remember reading in *Christianity Today* magazine a theologian's account of going into a high-school gymnasium to play basketball. The elderly janitor sat leaning against the door, reading a book. It was the Bible.

The author asked him, "What are you reading?"

"The Book of Revelation," the janitor replied.

"Do you know what it means?"

"Yep."

This intrigued the author-theologian, so he asked, "What does it mean?"

The answer was clear and terse: "It means Jesus is gonna win."

Right on.

"Write the vision plain." The proud are in big trouble. Sin will be judged.

The wrap-up will be no contest. Christ *will* be back and He *will* be Lord.

Unfortunately, a lot of people are falling down on the job because they don't believe that or don't know it. Many stumble in their faith because they can't handle the discrepancies of this life. It doesn't seem fair.

Why do the righteous suffer? The question echoes through the ages, through the Book of Job, bouncing around in Psalm 73, and is still on the minds of Old Testament prophets and New Testament apostles.

And the answer is plain—not that we can understand it all. God is in charge; He is not being fooled; all things will be made right, and there is coming an end.

In the meantime, the just can live by faith—in fact, we must!

In the meantime, we can run with endurance, looking at Jesus, who also went through some tough times but came out victorious.

"Write the vision plain." Let others know exactly how it is going to be, in kind and gentle and clear ways.

There are some obvious implications here for the pastor or the teacher. Leaders of God's flock are not put in such positions just to do theological jargon, or to impress their listeners. Instead their job is to help people really understand what God is saying.

But the application is for all of us. By the way we live, and by the simplicity of the message we share when we seek to witness—"Write the vision plain."

So that others may run.

It is a beautiful summer evening in America, and the smell of barbecued chicken and burgers is coming through the backyard hedges and fences. The splash and laughter of children can be heard at some of the homes in the neighborhood, and a satisfied couple in their forties starts an early evening walk around the block.

They see the family across the street backing the car out of the driveway. "There they go," Mr. Average says, "just like clockwork."

"I don't understand, and I guess I don't really want to," the Mrs. admits. "If going to church on an evening like this were all I had to do, I think I would start drinking."

"Maybe the hard stuff?"

"Maybe the hard stuff."

"Well, you have to give them credit for being disciplined," he says. "We could set our watches by their leaving at 5:35 on Sunday evenings and 6:35 on Wednesdays."

So the Averages admire, but clearly from a distance. She adds, "I can't imagine what it is they do at church once every Sunday, let alone going back for seconds in the evening!"

"Must be the nature of some churches. We always called them holy rollers when I was little."

The Faithfuls, who are now getting on the freeway to make the 6:00 evening service on time, are having their own conversation. Theirs is about the Averages.

"I saw them going out for an evening walk as we pulled away," she begins. "The Averages—what are their first names?"

"I forget now," says Mr. Faithful. "I think he works downtown."

"Sometimes I pity them because they must be so empty, and other times I envy them because our schedules are often so full, especially on Sundays."

"What do people do who don't go to church?"

"Looks like some of them take walks."

And so the Grand Chasm remains. It is one of the wonders of the modern world—that so many people can really know the Lord and be faithful to Him, but that the average observer can have such an inadequate understanding of the Gospel, and of why Christ came, and of grace itself.

But the story could be repeated in thousands of neighborhoods across America—even in smaller villages and towns, not just the big cities.

Most non-Christians have a little exposure to church or the Gospel, but no inside understanding. And the chasm gets wider as believers and unbelievers go their separate ways.

Untouched by each other.

Oh, occasionally the Faithfuls invite the Averages to a service or special meeting, but that would be something like my being invited to a monthly meeting of the Shriners by a 32nd degree Mason.

I would be scared to death.

Actually, I don't sense any need to be or even see a Mason in action, and my preconceived notions are such that I would have negative vibes mostly, neutral ones at best.

This is not to put down Shriners—I love the Tournament of Roses Parade! And I know very little about them.

But that is exactly the parallel! The Grand Chasm is the saddest part of all in the spiritual-secular situation in America.

The two sides barely know each other, and they misjudge each other constantly.

Athletes and non-athletes do it all the time too, but there it doesn't really matter. God probably cares very little who runs and who doesn't (as long as we get some kind of exercise)!

In the issue of everlasting life, however, it is very significant.

God told Habakkuk something He would certainly want us to know too: "Write the vision plain, so the people can run."

"Put it on a billboard, so people can notice."

"Use big letters and little words so readers get what you're saying."

We must leave our Christian hieroglyphics behind and learn to talk "neighborhood," or to speak the language they all speak at the office.

Certainly I'm not talking about the four-letter words or the morally dirty stuff, but just the same language.

We send our missionaries off to France or Timbuktu or Brazil and commission them to, above all, learn the language of the people and get to know them.

Build bridges!

I was talking with Wally Geiger, a missionary our church supports in Paris. "I really felt like an outsider the few days I was there," I said. "The attitude I picked up was, 'What are you doing here, buddy?' "

Wally was kind, but quick: "That's because you didn't know the language. Most Frenchmen will respond if they see you're really trying to learn and use their language."

It's no different here.

The response may not be saving acceptance, but we at least have so much more of a chance for a hearing when we know our neighbors and coworkers and are willing to be their friends.

Not just their witnesses.

The late Joe Bayly was always a bit ahead of his time and

peers with his wit and pointed-but-kind shots at our sacred cows in evangelicalism. In his satire, *The Gospel Blimp*, written long before the "friendship evangelism" emphasis, Bayly told about Christians who labored so hard to win their neighbors to the Lord that they launched a blimp, from which they broadcast the Gospel and dropped tract bombs.

Indeed, the neighbors came to Christ for grace and salvation, but it was not the frequent flights of the friendly "Goodforever" blimp that turned their hearts. That tactic did more to turn their stomachs!

It was another group of Christians who befriended their neighbors during fishing trips who got the message of love across.

That message usually flows better across kitchen tables and during office coffee breaks and on car rides after the game. Not that it can't flow from the pulpit or through the airwaves.

"Write the vision plain," Habakkuk was told. "So people can run."

Most people don't run because they can't really even say where the race is or where it is going!

I thought of this when our next-door neighbors were out for one of those evening walks I was talking about—not a Sunday or Wednesday or Thursday (visitation and board night) or I would have been gone for sure—and Jeanine and I ran to the front walk to greet and talk with them.

"If God was Jesus' Father, who was His mother?" she asked.

Oh, it wasn't her first question, to be sure. But it never would have come up if we had not been a part of their lives at least a bit, or if my wife were not so into getting to know the people right around us as well as the people at church.

And the added advantage is that we get to know some very nice people!

Joe Aldrich, Jim Petersen, and Becky Pippert have done

us all a trinity of favors with their books calling for friendship evangelism as well as proclamational evangelism.

It's certainly not either-or!

Those books—*Life-Style Evangelism, Evangelism for Our Generation*, and *Out of the Salt Shaker*—are candid and compelling.

The point is clear and can hardly be disputed: we have a lot of religion going on in America, but an awful lot of people are not getting the point.

All that many non-Christians would acknowledge is that we Christians live in a different world.

A world that is sometimes too busy in its own swirl of activities and superstars.

We have our own favorite singers and stand-up comedians and talk-show hosts and clichés and unspoken requests. But often we make no love inroads into unbelievers' lives, and their spirits remain untouched.

Mr. and Mrs. Average look at the Gospel and the evangelical church, at best, something like I look at the Lions Club—it's great if you have the time and want to participate. But, no thank you.

Now if I would spend some time—some good time—with a Lion, and hear how much fun the meetings are, or how being one has been special for him, I might try a Lion lunch or two.

What's a Christian to do?

I think we all know. We just have to stop talking about it and start doing it.

Let's keep the church services. I love it when the Christian runners all come together on Sundays to sing the running songs and talk about the finish line and encourage each other.

I even enjoy the Sunday evening time.

But let's also encourage each other to build bridges to

our friends and relatives and coworkers.

Maybe to join Lions.

Not to get someone's scalp, but to show love and express the goodness of God and hopefully talk, naturally and appropriately, about what Jesus Christ has done for us.

And they will be able to tell, for they will have seen the Gospel alive in our lives.

If it were just a matter of content, we could write the vision plain just by giving out the fabulous Christian literature that is everywhere or getting them to tune into Swindoll or MacArthur on the radio or Robertson or Falwell on the tube.

But content is not always the issue.

At least not just the facts.

Many people got the facts when they were little. "My mom made me go to church when we were little, and I've had enough for the rest of my life," one man told me.

Another: "I saw so much hypocrisy at church that you'll never get me back there."

And: "If Charlie's a Christian, the way he treats me, I don't want any part of it."

The Chasm widens.

Yet the race goes on, and many of us who run really love following Christ, and really do have something to share with the non-runners.

But we have to get alongside them a bit!

Jesus did.

Not without criticism, of course, but that did not seem to stop Him.

"Friend of winebibbers," some jeered. The religious sort, they had strong feelings about going down the steps of the caste system and mixing.

But He did.

He did indeed.

He wrote the vision plain.

I was nowhere near His level, but He came down to mine.

Such is salvation.

12

FINISHING THE COURSE

"I have fought the good fight, I have finished the course, I have kept the faith; in the future there is laid up for me the crown of righteousness, which the Lord, the righteous Judge, will award to me on that day; and not only to me, but also to all who have loved His appearing."

(2 Tim. 4:7-8)

Everyone knows about the agony of defeat. But there is also agony in victory. The winner sometimes has worked the hardest and agonized the longest.

And he feels the best.

This book has been about the agony of running, but also the joy of the race.

What could be a better thrill than to stand at the end of life and say, "I have agonized the good agony."

"I have fought the good fight."

"I have finished the course. I have kept the faith."

That's quite a way to go. And it is a prize available to all who wish.

That gives me hope.

Maybe you've heard the story of the most lopsided football game ever played, when mighty Georgia Tech beat tiny Cumberland College, 220-0.

I think that was the game where the Cumberland quarterback tossed a short but errant lateral to the halfback. The quarterback yelled, "Pick it up, pick it up!"

But the halfback had other ideas. "*You* pick it up; you dropped it."

It's easy to lose drive in life. Many Christians are sitting on the sidelines counting splinters in their backsides.

Or sitting on pews counting mistakes in the pastor's sermons.

Or thinking back about how they used to experience real joy in the Christian life and wondering what went wrong.

Such is the dropout way.

You've probably heard that man's greatest ability is not his ability to think, but to rationalize.

To excuse himself for going to the sidelines, at times.

Paul's life was often one of agony. Hard work.

But I imagine that at the end of the day he felt good. At least, he felt good in the inward sense—that he had done God's will in the twenty-four hours just ended.

We are not called to win the world.

Messianic complex or not, we are not responsible for everyone.

I am to finish *my* course.

You, yours.

That's it.

That's quite enough, for sure—a guaranteed lifetime job.

But it certainly beats carrying the burden of the world on your back or never being able to close your briefcase or to go home without an anxious sigh.

It certainly beats staying awake at night and wondering what else you should have done that day.

Finish your course. Do what you choose each day, be glad that God has given you those choices, and then go to sleep.

Maybe you heard the story about the guy who couldn't rest because he had so much of the weight of the world on his shoulders. Finally God told him to try to catch some shut-eye. "I can try to handle things during the night, at least," offered the Lord.

God can handle life all the time. He can use *all* of us effectively in furthering His Kingdom. And He can stretch our worlds and our spirits in the process.

There is nothing so satisfying as finishing a footrace. When you run like I do, it's not ribbon time, and because of my scruples, it's not Miller time.

It's just plain satisfaction time. You've finished the course.

On the hill back there at mile three you thought sure you would quit. In fact, you almost did.

You saw others who dropped out, all with satisfied looks on their faces. They were done. Early. Too early.

But you kept going. Or rather I did.

I finished. And am I glad!

That's Paul's sentiment too, sitting there in lock, stock, and barnacle.

He's about to lose his life, he tells Timothy. "I am already being poured out as a drink offering" (2 Tim. 4:6) is a euphemism for saying, "I'm about to die."

But still he is satisfied. He is finishing well.

That's what I need. In all the struggles of life, and with all the alternatives and the things that could ruin it, that's what I need. To finish the course with personal satisfaction and the satisfaction of Christ. To blink my eyes, wake up in heaven, and say, "I made it. With His grace and by His help, I made it home in style!"

It doesn't matter what the ribbons look like or how many crowns I get to stack. It matters that it was for His glory and that I ran as fast as I could and felt His pleasure as I ran.

Fight the *good* fight! Agonize the *good* agony.

There are countless agonies you can agonize. You can go for the money. You can go for political prestige. You can try hedonism. You can make sex or thoughts about it the main passion of life.

But Paul says in essence, "I have agonized the good agony." As opposed to the bad agonies or the mediocre agonies or the pretty decent agonies.

Even church is not enough of an agony to agonize with all your days. Religion itself is a great vehicle and a way to serve. The system can be helpful. But if it's not the good fight to know Christ and to get Him known and to really grow in your love for Him, it's not the best agony.

If we are going to go to a lot of trouble in this life to get good at something, it might as well be to get good at the best.

To glorify God.

That is the highest goal.

That is the best thing.

Surface Christianity comes cheap and looks impressive.

We can get people to raise their hands in seven minutes and be done with it.

We can catch people who will volunteer once, and put them all in a church, and have something great for about a week or so.

Concerts we can fill.

We can show off a Christian celebrity and pack out a banquet, especially if the desserts are free.

But let's face it, what we really need—and what God really wants—is endurance.

We need people who grind out the days, even when they don't feel like serving others.

We need people who can last under pain, and be willing to stay at just that spot—under it—until something better comes along from God.

We need shovelers and diggers and runners and plodders and helpers and handymen.

People who will stay with what is right, no matter what the alternatives or consequences.

We need endurance. We need endurers.

Runners who can go to the end. People who will follow Christ with lasting results.

Like the ones who spend years with the Muslims and see just a few converts, but endure because they know they are in Christ's spot.

Like Job, who was under the worst of pains, but didn't try to escape by renouncing his Creator.

Like my grandmother, who until the end of her days confessed faith in Christ, despite the pain of death and anguish and misunderstandings and strokes.

Enduring means you really believe it. Enduring means you don't think anything is more important than your faith, and no one more significant than Christ.

Endurance is what we need.

"Run with endurance," Hebrews 12 says.

Most runners don't have to work hard for the big race. What I mean by that statement is that so much adrenalin is flowing because of the headlines or the natural competition that it's almost impossible to be mentally down. It's the practice where runners need to be psyched up to be faithful.

All of us are that way. We're ready on the big moments to obey the Lord and give Him our lives. Everybody prays before surgery.

It's another thing to give thanks for the daily. To operate on the basis of obedience all the time, to finish the course.

That's what Christian running is all about. The very daily. The momentary. Not just the eternal.

Whatever good thing gets you psyched up, use it. It may be a word from a friend. It may be a psalm or another portion of Scripture. It may be just a moment of meditation. But then go to the dinner table and give of yourself to your family. Then go to a neighbor and show God's love. Then get ready for the daily stuff.

When we are faithful in the daily, the big event of life—death—will come rather easily.

If I know the Lord on a daily basis, and I'm not frightened by Him now, I will not be frightened at the big meeting. He will not be the grand old man upstairs or the guardian angel or even just the Great Physician. He will be my friend.

I will be ready.

Bring it on.

But in the meantime, bring on the daily. And with the daily routine, daily obedience.

Such is life.

Maybe it's nice now and then to run with pizzazz.

There are people who run well with color.

Fine at a given time.

But run with endurance. Be loyal today and loyal in seven years.

Have a good marriage today and a better one in ten.

Do your work well today and even better tomorrow.

We need endurance.

We need people to believe Jesus Christ is Lord of yesterday, today, and tomorrow.

Many people are willing to celebrate forgiveness and really jump up and down about guilt being gone, but we must also take the accompanying command, "Go and sin no more," and run with it.

Let's hear it for the finishers.

Let's hear it for the people who run the long race.

Let's celebrate those men and women up in years who have been faithful to Jesus Christ for decades and continue to do His thing.

Let's hear it for the spiritual survivors, the ones who don't always hear bells ringing within their hearts, but who endure and do what is right and keep on going.

Sometimes they feel like it; sometimes they don't.

But they take another step.

Such is faith. Such is Jesus' desire.

That's why Hebrews 12:2 (KJV) says, "Looking unto Jesus the author and finisher of our faith." Underline *finisher*.

"Perfecter."

"Completer."

Watch Him and you won't see someone sitting down on the side and threatening to give up.

Fix your eyes on Him and you won't pull over to the side in this race called life.

Keep running.

To the end.

And the finish line will be something else!

For victory in the Olympic games of ancient Greece, each champion received an olive wreath. And he became an idol in his home city.

Usually he received a free home, meals "on the house"

for a lifetime, and large sums of money. Often a street in the city was named for him. Maybe he even endorsed Wheaties!

When Diagoras, the father of Pherenice, won his Olympic championship, he was told, "Die, Diagoras, for thou hast nothing short of divinity to desire."

Cheating was scorned. Athletes who violated the Olympic code had to erect statues, called Zanes, at the foot of Mount Kronius.

There is so much more of a prize, and so much more at stake, in the race of life. The finish will be glorious for those who do not cheat!

"Train yourself to be godly," Paul exhorts believers (1 Tim. 4:7, NIV).

Peter talks about unbelievers as just the opposite, people "trained in greed" (2 Peter 2:14).

Such men and women get really good at being selfish because they work at it all the time. They get the gold in greed—first place.

America's great marathon hope at the 1972 Olympics in Munich was Frank Shorter. The color commentator for U.S. television was Eric Segal, and he was obviously sure of Shorter's victory chances.

But when the first runner came through the underpass and emerged into the stadium for the final lap, Segal wondered aloud, "Who is that? It's not Shorter—who is it?"

Then, after a pause, he started yelling into the microphone, "He's a fake! Get him out of there! He's a fake!"

The man on the track was enjoying his brief moment of glory. The ovation was loud. Everyone was standing (and wondering who he was!).

But sure enough, he was a fraud. Soon the public address announcer said in German, "Get him off. He is not true. Take him off." And the stadium guards caught the fellow and took him away.

It was later learned that the imposter had jumped off the

back of a soft drink delivery truck that had just driven through the stadium underpass. He then ran in, pretending to be dog-tired and triumphant.

He had his day, or rather moment, as do many who break the rules and seem to get away with it. But no one really does get away with it in the end.

Follow the rules. It will get you on the winners' platform with people like Paul, who said, "I have finished the course, I have kept the faith" (2 Tim. 4:7).

And because Paul played by the rules, he could go on to write, "In the future there is laid up for me the crown of righteousness, which the Lord, the righteous Judge, will award to me on that day" (v. 8).

Our goal is the same.

I saw and here reprint one marathon runner's description of what it's like to run in a marathon. See if you can catch his feelings:

> The start of the marathon is joyous. After all those weeks of training, anticipation, and anxiety, the physical release of beginning the race is a pure high. Like children rushing out for recess. We're finally moving!
>
> Some children in the yard up ahead are holding up a hand-lettered sign. It says "Baskin-Robbins, One Mile." I wonder what would happen if all the would-be marathoners decided to forget the whole thing and just go eat ice cream. Would it spoil some vast eternal plan? Maybe it would.
>
> Ten miles and all's well. Try not to subtract 10 from 26, if you can help it.
>
> The runners aren't talking and laughing now. Everyone seems to be absorbed in his own personal struggle.
>
> Twenty-one miles. Yes, Virginia, there is a

wall. It's alive and well and living in Michigan. It just keeps falling on me. Not one big crash, just a whole bunch of little ones. The ceiling and floors are crumbling too. The whole building has been condemned. Can a condemned building run five more miles?

There are a lot of people walking up ahead. Does the universe care if you stop and walk in a marathon? Do I care? If I stop and walk, will the earth stop revolving around the sun or something?

Four more miles, or is it four more light-years?

Henderson says you're supposed to let the other runners carry you through the last part of the race. That sounds like a good idea, but there aren't many runners around now. There are some walkers, but they don't help. They discourage me. There's one runner up ahead in a yellow T-shirt. On the back the word "DUMMY" is printed in big blue letters. Does that mean him or me? It could work either way; grinding out the last four miles with a big blue "DUMMY" sign jiggling up in front of me. Now he's slowing down. Don't stop. If you pull me in, I'll push you in. Fair enough? He's walking. I'll have to pass him. Goodbye, Brother Dummy! See you in the shower.

The water tower is getting closer, though. It's not a mirage. There's an end to this somewhere. Somewhere on the other side of infinite distance, infinite time. Maybe when I finish, I can lie down and drink the water tower until it's dry. Or maybe they can carry me to the top and throw me in.

But I have to finish. That's not a choice. I have to finish. I don't know why. I don't care why. Burn what you have to, body, just let me finish. Burn it in the runner's internal fires and send the smoke out the runner's chimney.

Twenty-five miles. Just past the timers, there's a nice looking girl. She asks me if I want some ice. Her smile reflects concern and compassion.

We're going to make it, Old Paint! We're going home, Mangy Moose! Just don't fall down. If I fall down, six men and a crane won't get me up.

Twenty-six miles. Only the stupid 385 yards to go. I think the extra yards came in because some Queen of England didn't want to move to watch an Olympic marathon.

I'll finish now. The rest of it could be barbed wire and broken glass and I'd crawl over it somehow. I'd rather finish running, though.

Here's the track. It's almost over. Oh what a beautiful sight! There's a great big "FINISH" banner to run under. There are people there and some kind of music. If marathoners have a heaven, it must be something like this.

The parallels to the Christian life are obvious, but allow me to note them for you anyway:

The start of the Christian life is joyous. After all those years of fighting faith, the spiritual release of beginning the race is a pure high. Like children rushing out for recess, we're finally saved.

Some people at work are trying to get me to forget Sundays and join their sports club, and they laugh at my faith. I wonder what would happen if all Christians decided to forget the whole thing and just go sit around. Would it spoil some vast eternal plan? Maybe it would. For sure.

Ten years and all's well. Try not to think about all the possible temptations, if you can help it.

Tests hit. Not everyone is talking and laughing now. Some have dropped out or fallen back.

Now and then a wall hits. Satan makes inroads. Life seems like it isn't even worth it. For a few days you even forget that you have the Holy Spirit. It's scary. But you get back to trusting . . . and the running and serving happens again.

A lot of people walking now. In fact, some of the people who got you started in this Christian life are walking; some of them are even sitting down. They got tired, they say. A few invite you to join them in the shade. But you can't because you hear the voice of the Lord in the Scriptures calling you. Somehow, in your mind's eye, you see Him running, enduring the worst of affliction, taking even the pain of the cross for you, and you want to go on. You ask for the control of His Spirit and you get going . . . doing what is right.

There's one runner up ahead with the word "HYPOCRITE" printed in big blue letters on his back. Does he mean me or him? It could work either way. Now he's slowing down. He's walking. I'll have to pass him. Goodbye, Brother Hypocrite!

The end is getting closer. I know Christ will be back someday. Maybe when He comes, I can lie down and drink from the water of life forever, in the presence of Jesus Christ Himself.

I have to finish. It's a choice, but I have chosen. I know why—because of all Christ has done for me, and the beauty of the finish!

I'll finish now. The rest of the race could be tests of all kinds, but I know the Lord will give grace and strength. I'm going to make it!

Here's the finish banner, and Christ is back! What a sight—and *some* kind of music!

There's my mother . . . and my sister . . . hello, hello! There's David! And Paul! And all the saints!

Jesus, my Lord, I love You!

Yes, someday I will finish the race we call life. Maybe before you get this book. Maybe in a few years. Maybe in fifty.

But I will cross the finish line. And He will be there.

I will struggle across.

I am no flash. Made of clay, I will have my scabs. But my heart is His, and my growth is through Him. I have kept running so far, and will continue to the end.

And He will open up His arms. I will break the tape, not beating anybody, but finishing nonetheless. Everyone gets the prize in this race.

So run, that you may win.

So finish, that you may exalt Him.

So go to the end, that you may sing along the way and especially at the finish.

How do I imagine the finish? Banners. Songs of joy.

They're singing the Hallelujah Chorus, and He is there.

It is His day, but it is my day too. By sheer love He has decided to share it with me. It is a crowning day. It is a finish day. It is the end of the line. And the start of eternity.

Whether by death or at His coming, it is triumph. It is our transportation, a run, into His presence. I shout.

I feel the joy of crossing that finish line when I try a nine-miler, only this one will be 500 times as strong.

He opens His arms. I fall into them. He hugs.

I am home. The race is over.

We win.

THE GOLD

I recently read about Bob Wieland, last and first in the 1986 New York City Marathon.

He finished last—19,413th.

But he was the first to ever run a marathon with his arms instead of his legs.

Wieland is a forty-year-old Californian—also a Christian—whose legs were blown off in a Vietnam War battle seventeen years ago.

He finished the New York race in four days, two hours, forty-eight minutes, seventeen seconds. That's the slowest time in marathon history, but maybe the best.

Wieland can go about a mile an hour, using his muscular arms like crutches to swing his torso forward. He sits on a fifteen-pound "saddle" and covers his fists with pads he calls his "size-one running shoes."

"The first step was the most difficult," Wieland said. "After that, we were on our way home.

"The joy has been the journey."

If he can do that—and finish—we can run the marathon of faith.

Yes—and finish.

And what a fabulous finish it will be.

No question about it, the winners' platform is wide enough for all of us and will make the whole race make sense.

Heaven.

The place where the glory of the Lord shines without the fog of selfishness.

Bill Broadhurst was trying to run a 10K race in Omaha. Broadhurst's hero, the famous runner, Bill Rodgers, would win the race in less than thirty minutes. Broadhurst, on the other hand, because of an aneurysm on the right side of his brain resulting in a crippled left side, would struggle from beginning to end.

He was dragging after an hour and it was worse at an hour and a half. Some kids yelled out, "Hey, mister, you missed the race!" They didn't understand. Broadhurst's whole left side was almost numb.

He wanted to quit, but decided he must keep going. A born-again Christian, Broadhurst later said that the verse, "I buffet my body and make it my slave," kept running through his mind.

It was a day with his hero, and he, like Rodgers, must go to the end.

The traffic was back in the streets again. Aching and discouraged, Broadhurst had to make his own way—alone.

Two hours. What did it matter? Why bother to finish?

Two hours and twenty minutes. Finally he saw down the street to where the finish banner had been. By now, everyone was gone. The banner was down.

Why finish?

But Broadhurst said he answered that tension inside with drive and discipline. The great human race is a marathon, not a sprint, and calls for a finish. Not necessarily a blaze of glory, but a finish.

Broadhurst would. He must. He did.

Literally pulling himself step by painful step, he

approached the final yards.

Than it happened.

From out of the shadows of an alleyway nearby stepped a small crowd of people.

In front: Bill Rodgers.

He had learned Broadhurst's story and had waited for this special moment.

Broadhurst stumbled across the finish line and into the arms of his hero and now friend, Bill Rodgers.

A hug.

The tears.

The joy.

Rodgers took the ribbon holding the gold medal off his own neck and placed it around Bill Broadhurst's. "You are the winner," he said.

"Take the gold."

And my mind goes to the day we stumble across the finish line. With all our handicaps spiritually, with a thousand real and imagined fears, with failures for sure. But we cross that line and He gives us the gold.

The golden gift of heaven.

Nice!

Such is eternal life.